4

Speak NOW

COMMUNICATE with CONFIDENCE

Mari Vargo

OXFORD
UNIVERSITY PRESS

Welcome to 

Communicate *with* Confidence

Communicating with confidence means expressing yourself accurately, fluently, and appropriately. **English in Action** lessons throughout the Student Book present video clips which show students how to use target language in real-life settings. The video is available through Oxford Learn Online Practice, DVD, and on the iTools Classroom Presentation Software CD-ROM.

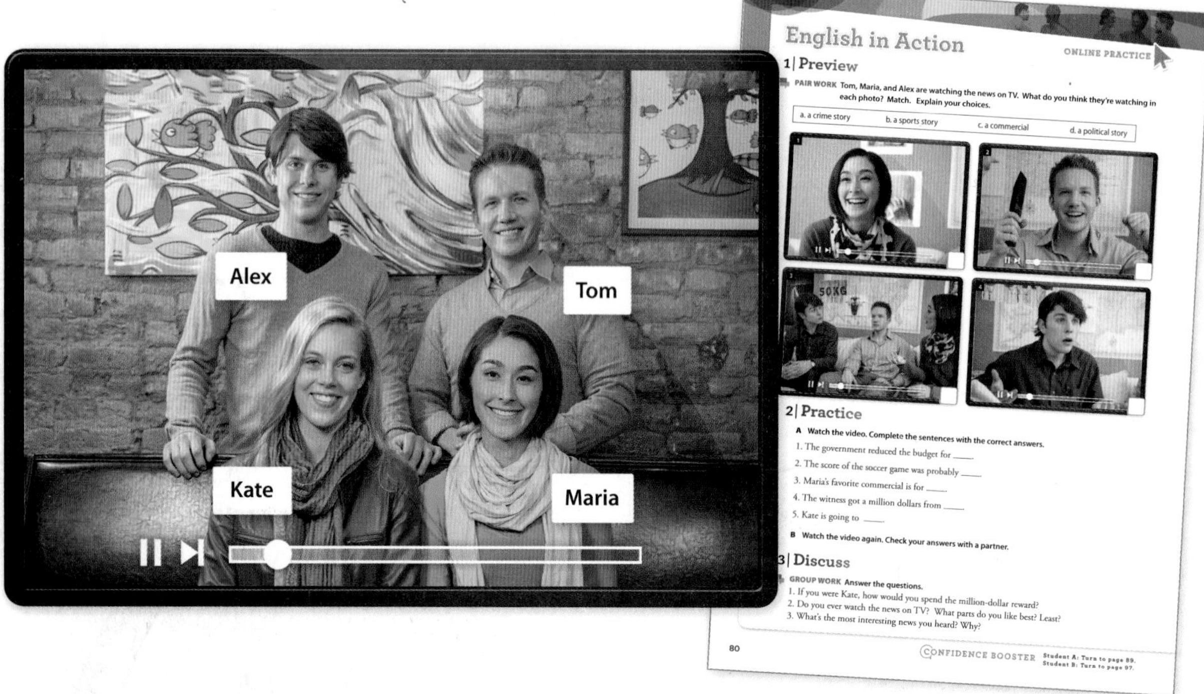

English in Action

ONLINE PRACTICE

1 | Preview

PAIR WORK Tom, Maria, and Alex are watching the news on TV. What do you think they're watching in each photo? Match. Explain your choices.

a. a crime story b. a sports story c. a commercial d. a political story

2 | Practice

A Watch the video. Complete the sentences with the correct answers.

1. The government reduced the budget for ____
2. The score of the soccer game was probably ____
3. Maria's favorite commercial is for ____
4. The witness got a million dollars from ____
5. Kate is going to ____

B Watch the video again. Check your answers with a partner.

3 | Discuss

GROUP WORK Answer the questions.

1. If you were Kate, how would you spend the million-dollar reward?
2. Do you ever watch the news on TV? What parts do you like best? Least?
3. What's the most interesting news you heard? Why?

80 CONFIDENCE BOOSTER Student A: Turn to page 99. Student B: Turn to page 97.

Online Practice powered by oxfordlearn

Speak Now Online Practice features over 100 engaging self-study activities to help you improve your speaking, pronunciation, and listening skills.

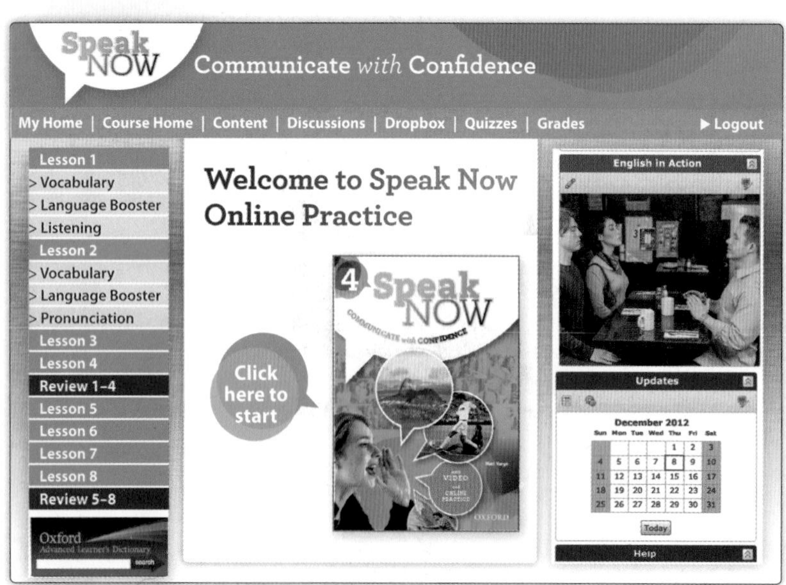

Use the **access card** on the inside back cover to log in at www.oxfordlearn.com/login.

Maximize Speaking

Every activity in every lesson includes a speaking task to ensure students maximize their opportunity to develop confident conversation skills. In each two-page lesson, students learn key **Vocabulary**, practice these new words and develop structured speaking skills through the **Conversation** activity, study new functional language in the **Language Booster** section, and then develop either **Pronunciation** or **Listening** skills in preparation for a communicative **Speak with Confidence** activity.

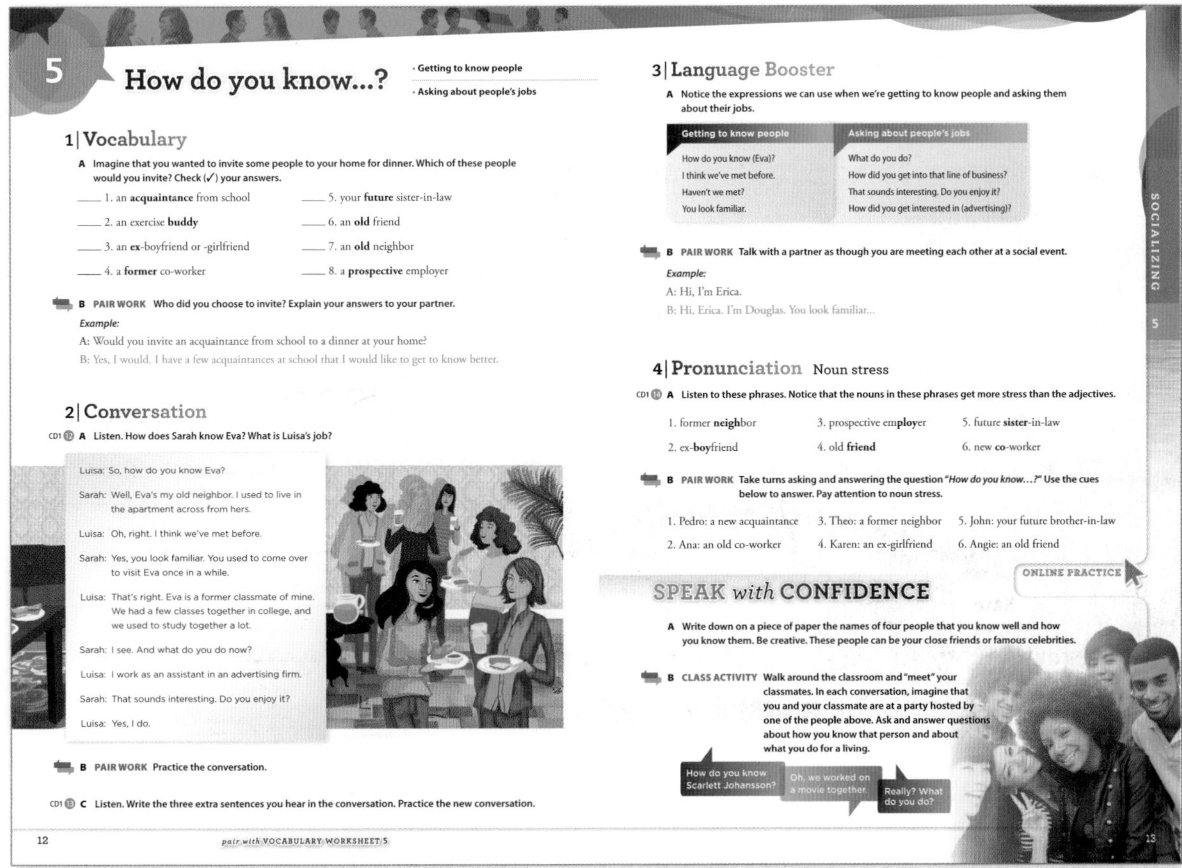

5 How do you know...?

- Getting to know people
- Asking about people's jobs

1 | Vocabulary

A Imagine that you wanted to invite some people to your home for dinner. Which of these people would you invite? Check (✓) your answers.

___ 1. an **acquaintance** from school
___ 2. an exercise **buddy**
___ 3. an **ex**-boyfriend or -girlfriend
___ 4. a **former** co-worker
___ 5. your **future** sister-in-law
___ 6. an **old** friend
___ 7. an **old** neighbor
___ 8. a **prospective** employer

B PAIR WORK Who did you choose to invite? Explain your answers to your partner.

Example:
A: Would you invite an acquaintance from school to a dinner at your home?
B: Yes, I would. I have a few acquaintances at school that I would like to get to know better.

2 | Conversation

CD1 A Listen. How does Sarah know Eva? What is Luisa's job?

Luisa: So, how do you know Eva?
Sarah: Well, Eva's my old neighbor. I used to live in the apartment across from hers.
Luisa: Oh, right. I think we've met before.
Sarah: Yes, you look familiar. You used to come over to visit Eva once in a while.
Luisa: That's right. Eva is a former classmate of mine. We had a few classes together in college, and we used to study together a lot.
Sarah: I see. And what do you do now?
Luisa: I work as an assistant in an advertising firm.
Sarah: That sounds interesting. Do you enjoy it?
Luisa: Yes, I do.

B PAIR WORK Practice the conversation.

CD1 C Listen. Write the three extra sentences you hear in the conversation. Practice the new conversation.

3 | Language Booster

A Notice the expressions we can use when we're getting to know people and asking them about their jobs.

Getting to know people	Asking about people's jobs
How do you know (Eva)?	What do you do?
I think we've met before.	How did you get into that line of business?
Haven't we met?	That sounds interesting. Do you enjoy it?
You look familiar.	How did you get interested in (advertising)?

B PAIR WORK Talk with a partner as though you are meeting each other at a social event.

Example:
A: Hi, I'm Erica.
B: Hi, Erica. I'm Douglas. You look familiar...

4 | Pronunciation Noun stress

CD1 A Listen to these phrases. Notice that the nouns in these phrases get more stress than the adjectives.

1. former **neighbor**
2. ex-**boy**friend
3. prospective em**ploy**er
4. old **friend**
5. future **sis**ter-in-law
6. new **co**-worker

B PAIR WORK Take turns asking and answering the question *"How do you know...?"* Use the cues below to answer. Pay attention to noun stress.

1. Pedro: a new acquaintance
2. Ana: an old co-worker
3. Theo: a former neighbor
4. Karen: an ex-girlfriend
5. John: your future brother-in-law
6. Angie: an old friend

ONLINE PRACTICE

SPEAK *with* CONFIDENCE

A Write down on a piece of paper the names of four people that you know well and how you know them. Be creative. These people can be your close friends or famous celebrities.

B CLASS ACTIVITY Walk around the classroom and "meet" your classmates. In each conversation, imagine that you and your classmate are at a party hosted by one of the people above. Ask and answer questions about how you know that person and about what you do for a living.

SOCIALIZING 5

12 *pair with* VOCABULARY WORKSHEET 5 13

Self-Assessment

Through the **Speak Now** lessons, learners evaluate their progress through role-play situations inspired by the Can-Do statements of the Common European Framework (CEFR).

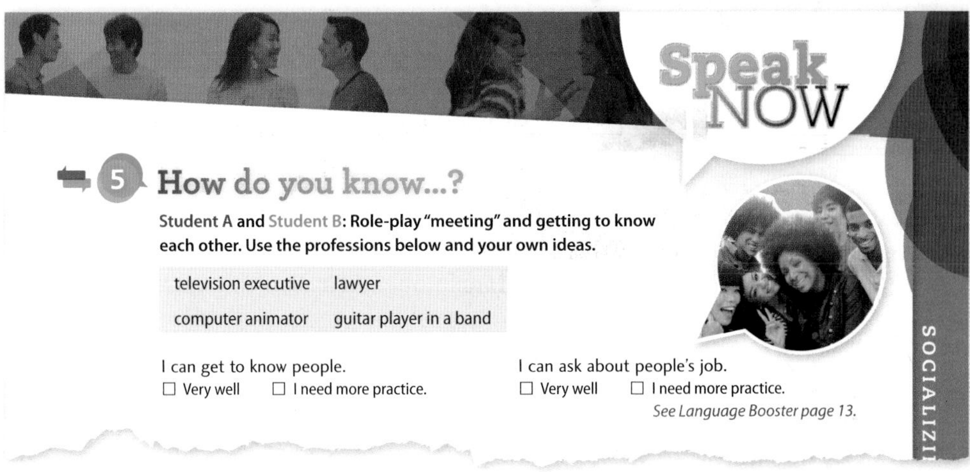

5 How do you know...?

Student A and Student B: Role-play "meeting" and getting to know each other. Use the professions below and your own ideas.

television executive	lawyer
computer animator	guitar player in a band

I can get to know people.
☐ Very well ☐ I need more practice.

I can ask about people's job.
☐ Very well ☐ I need more practice.
See Language Booster page 13.

SOCIALIZI

Scope and Sequence

Scope and Sequence

1 I learned a lot from...

- Asking about significant experiences
- Talking about important events

1 | Vocabulary

A Look at the phrases below. Check each thing that has happened to you in the last five years.

_____ overcome an obstacle

_____ get into (a new interest)

_____ have a setback

_____ have an/the opportunity to (do something you wanted to do)

_____ face a challenge

_____ make a change

_____ make the decision to (do something different)

_____ take a risk

B PAIR WORK Take turns talking about the things that have happened to you. Ask two follow-up questions.

2 | Conversation

CD1 02 **A Listen. What happened to Louis recently? What happened to Kristin?**

Kristin: Hi, Louis. I hear you've made a big change recently.

Louis: Yeah, I have. I just got a job as a photographer. _____

Kristin: Oh, wow! How did you get into photography? _____

Louis: I had the opportunity to work with a photographer friend of mine. I learned a lot from working with him. I also learned that I wanted to be a professional photographer.

Kristin: That's great! Congratulations!

Louis: Thanks! Oh, that reminds me, Ana tells me that you just moved.

Kristin: Yes, I did. I had a setback last month when I lost my job, but it turned out to be the best thing that ever happened to me. I just got a much better job, and I moved to São Paulo. _____

Louis: I'm sorry to hear about your setback, but so glad to hear about your new job! _____

B PAIR WORK Practice the conversation. Then find the best places to add the sentences below to the conversation and practice it again.

1. I didn't realize you were a photographer.	3. I love it!
2. I hope I can visit!	4. I've always wanted to live there.

3 | Language Booster

A **Notice the different ways we ask about significant experiences and talk about important events.**

Asking about significant experiences	Talking about important events
I hear that / (Ana) tells me that — you just moved.	It is one of the most exciting things I've ever done.
Oh, that reminds me, (Ana tells me that you just moved).	It turned out to be the best thing that ever happened to me.
	It's the best decision I've ever made.
	It was one of the biggest challenges I've ever faced.

B **PAIR WORK** **Take turns asking and talking about an important event in your life.**

4 | Listening

CD1 03 **A** **Listen. Write the correct name under each picture.**

Clara	Alex	Victor	Larissa

a 

b 

c 

d 

______ ______ ______ ______

CD1 03 **B** **Listen again. Mark the statements T (true) or F (false). Then compare your answers with a partner.**

_____ 1. Clara wants to be a teacher.

_____ 2. Alex lost his job last month.

_____ 3. Victor is studying to become a baker.

_____ 4. Larissa got married last year.

ONLINE PRACTICE

SPEAK *with* CONFIDENCE

A **PAIR WORK** **Complete each story below with your own idea. Think of the most exciting and challenging things you can. Then share and respond to stories with your partner.**

1. I faced a challenge. ______________________________

2. I overcame an obstacle. ______________________________

3. I took a risk. I made the decision to ______________________________

B **GROUP WORK** **Join another pair and share and respond to stories.**

2 Did you hear about...?

- Introducing interesting stories
- Asking for details

1 | Vocabulary

A Complete the paragraph with the correct form of a verb in the box.

injure	pass out	react	respond	report	witness

Last week, there was a fire at a local school. A lot of people ____________ (1) the scene. They were worried because the fire kept growing. Luckily, fire fighters ____________ (2) very quickly. No one was ____________ (3) from the fire, but a witness was taken to the hospital. The news ____________ (4) that a woman ____________ (5) hysterically and couldn't take the excitement. She ____________ (6) in the middle of the street!

B PAIR WORK Tell your partner about something interesting you recently heard about.

2 | Conversation

CD1 04 **A Listen. How did the man fall onto the subway track? What did he do after he woke up?**

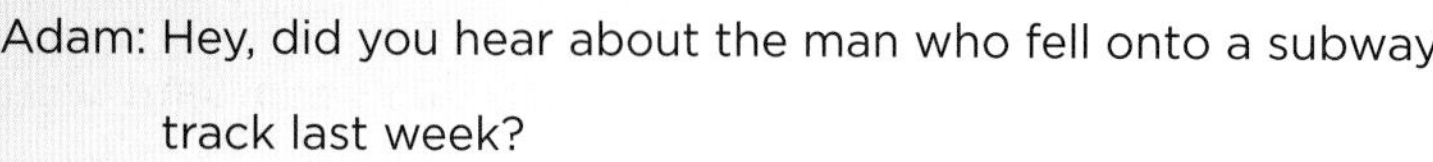

Adam: Hey, did you hear about the man who fell onto a subway track last week?

Teresa: No, how did that happen?

Adam: He was texting a friend, and he wasn't watching where he was going. He fell, hit his head, and passed out.

Teresa: No way. What happened next?

Adam: Luckily, someone witnessed the whole thing. He jumped onto the track and pulled the guy out.

Teresa: Wow! Did the guy injure himself in the fall?

Adam: Not really. The guy woke up after a few minutes, and he was fine. He got up and finished typing his text message!

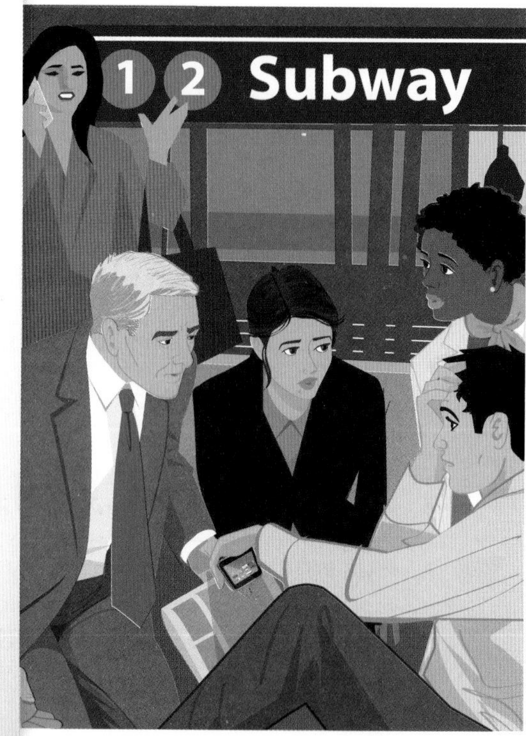

B PAIR WORK Practice the conversation.

CD1 05 **C Listen. Write the three extra sentences you hear in the conversation. Practice the new conversation.**

3 | Language Booster

A **Notice the ways we introduce interesting stories and ask for details.**

Introducing interesting stories	Asking for details
Did you hear about (the man who fell onto a subway track last week)?	So what did (he) do?
You'll never believe what happened.	How did (he) react?
You're not going to believe the story I heard.	How did that happen?
	What happened?

B **PAIR WORK** **Tell your partner an interesting story that you know.**

Examples:

A: You'll never believe what happened. My neighbors and I kept losing things, like keys and shoes.

B: How did that happen?

A: It turned out that the neighbor's new cat was taking things and hiding them in the basement!

PEOPLE 2

4 | Pronunciation Linking vowels in phrases

CD1 06 **A** **Listen to these phrases. Notice that any word that begins with a vowel inside a phrase links with the word before it.**

1. hear**d a**bout 2. t**o a** friend 3. the stor**y I** heard 4. passe**s o**ut

B **Complete the conversation below with your own ideas. Then circle the words that begin with vowels.**

A: Did you hear about the woman in California who ____________________.

B: What happened?

A: Well, this woman ____________________________.

C **PAIR WORK** **Practice the conversation with a partner.**

ONLINE PRACTICE

SPEAK with CONFIDENCE

A **PAIR WORK** **Work with a partner to make a list of interesting or unusual stories you've heard about recently.**

B **GROUP WORK** **Take turns telling the most interesting story to your group members.**

Did you hear about the company who held an office chair race?

No way! What happened?

C **CLASS ACTIVITY** **Present one story from your group. Choose the most interesting story from the class.**

3 I can't stand it when...

- Describing pet peeves
- Sympathizing

1 | Vocabulary

A Check (✓) the things that annoy you.

____ when people **interrupt** me	____ when salespeople are **rude**
____ when a server **ignores** me	____ when people **stare** at me
____ when people **chew** loudly	____ when people are **arrogant**
____ when people **leave** dirty dishes	____ when people have poor driving **etiquette**

B PAIR WORK Tell your partner about two of your pet peeves.

2 | Conversation

CD1 07 **A Listen. Why is Marco annoyed? What are other things that annoy Jenny and Marco?**

Marco: Hi, Jenny. I'm so annoyed.

Jenny: What's wrong, Marco? ____

Marco: I was just at the movies, and there was a guy there who talked through the whole thing. I can't stand it when people talk during a movie.

Jenny: Yeah, I know what you mean. It gets on my nerves when people are rude like that. But it really gets me when people text during a movie.

Marco: Yeah, I hear you. ____

Jenny: You know what else bugs me? I hate it when people chew their popcorn really loudly.

Marco: Me, too! Oh, and it bugs me when people leave their popcorn and sodas on the floor after the movie instead of throwing them away.

Jenny: Oh, same here! ____

Marco: Maybe we should just start watching movies at home from now on. ____

B PAIR WORK Practice the conversation. Then find the best places to add the sentences below to the conversation and practice it again.

1. That's one of my pet peeves, too.	3. We might get less annoyed.
2. You look upset.	4. People should turn their phones off in the theater.

3 | Language Booster

A **Notice the ways we describe pet peeves and sympathize with the other person.**

Describing pet peeves		Sympathizing
I hate it when I can't stand it when It bugs me when It gets on my nerves when	people chew loudly. people are rude.	Yeah, I know what you mean. I can't either. Same here. Yeah, I hear you.

B **PAIR WORK** **Take turns describing your biggest pet peeves.**

Examples:

A: So what's your one of your biggest pet peeves?

B: I can't stand it when my roommate leaves her clothes all over the apartment.

A: Yeah, I hear you.

B: How about you?

A: It bugs me when people are arrogant.

PEOPLE 3

4 | Listening

CD1 08 **A** **Listen to four people describe their pet peeves. Number the pictures from 1 to 4.**

a 

b 

c 

d 

CD1 08 **B** **Listen again. In each conversation, does the listener have the same pet peeve or not? Write *yes* or *no*.**

1. ____________ 2. ____________ 3. ____________ 4. ____________

ONLINE PRACTICE

SPEAK *with* CONFIDENCE

A **CLASS ACTIVITY** **Walk around the class. Ask your classmates, *"What's your biggest pet peeve?"* Write the person's name and his or her biggest pet peeve.**

Name	Pet peeve

B **GROUP WORK** **Share the three most interesting pet peeves you learned about your classmates.**

4 You put up with a lot.

- Making suggestions
- Commenting on suggestions

1 | Vocabulary

A Read the sentences about common friendship problems. Check (✓) the ones you have experienced.

_____ 1. Your friend seems to feel **awkward** around your other friends.

_____ 2. You **confront** your friend about a problem, and he or she gets angry and stops speaking to you.

_____ 3. Your friend wants to **hang out with** you all the time, but you have things to do.

_____ 4. Your friend **keeps** asking you to lend him or her money.

_____ 5. Your friend is **pushy** around your other friends and constantly interrupts them when they talk.

_____ 6. Your friend expects you to **put up with** his or her lateness, but gets upset when you are late.

_____ 7. Your friend lied to you, and you are beginning to **resent** him or her because of it.

B PAIR WORK Describe a problem you have had with a friend. Are you still friends with the person?

2 | Conversation

CD1 09 **A** Listen. Why isn't Pablo with Ingrid and Robert? What is Robert going to do?

Ingrid: Hi, Robert. Where's Pablo? I thought he was hanging out with us tonight.
Robert: Hi, Ingrid. He canceled at the last minute.
Ingrid: Again? You put up with a lot from him.

Robert: Yeah, he keeps doing it. I'm starting to resent him for it.
Ingrid: Have you tried confronting him about it?

Robert: Do you really think that's a good idea? I don't want to be pushy and have an awkward conversation.

Ingrid: If you don't feel comfortable talking to him, you might want to consider texting him about it.

Robert: That's not a bad idea. I'll give it a try.
Ingrid: Great! Let me know how it turns out.

B PAIR WORK Practice the conversation.

CD1 10 **C** Listen. Write the three extra sentences you hear in the conversation. Practice the new conversation.

3 | Language Booster

A **Notice the ways we make and comment on suggestions.**

Making suggestions		Commenting on suggestions
Have you thought about Have you tried	confronting him?	Do you really think that's a good idea? That might work. That's worth thinking about.
You might want to consider You might want to think about	texting him.	I'm not really sure that would work. That's not a bad idea.

B **PAIR WORK** **Share and give advice about the friendship problems below.**

My friend is ignoring me. My friend told my secret. My friend lied about me.

4 | Pronunciation Reduction of *have you*

CD1 11 **A** **Listen. Notice the way *have you* is reduced in these sentences to sound like *havya*.**

1. **Haveya** thought about asking her?
2. **Haveya** tried confronting him about it?
3. **Haveya** considered texting him?

B **PAIR WORK** **Share and give advice about the friendship problems in the Language Booster section, part B. This time, pay attention to your pronunciation of *have you*.**

ONLINE PRACTICE

SPEAK *with* CONFIDENCE

A **PAIR WORK** **Look at the friendship problems in the Vocabulary section. Think of a possible solution for each problem.**

My friend expects me to put up with his lateness, but gets upset when I am a few minutes late.

That's not fair. You might want to consider saying something to him.

B **GROUP WORK** **Describe a friendship problem to your group and respond to each person's advice. Then vote on the best piece of advice.**

English in Action

PEOPLE

1 2 3 4

VIDEO

1 | Preview

PAIR WORK **Look at the photos. Maria needs a new roommate. She is talking to Kate to see if she would be a good roommate. What do you think they are talking about? What questions would you ask Kate?**

2 | Practice

A Watch the video. Mark the statements T (true) or F (false).

_____ 1. Kate likes Maria's apartment. ______________________________

_____ 2. Kate is the first person that Maria has interviewed. ______________________________

_____ 3. Kate is upset because she lost her job. ______________________________

_____ 4. Maria has a new job. ______________________________

_____ 5. Kate didn't get along well with one of her old roommates. ______________________________

_____ 6. At the end, Maria thinks Kate is a wonderful roommate. ______________________________

B Watch the video again. Rewrite the false statements so they are true.

3 | Discuss

GROUP WORK **Answer the questions.**

1. Do you think Kate lied to Maria? Why or why not?
2. Do you agree with Tom's advice? What do you think Maria should do?
3. Have you ever had problems with people you live with? What kinds of problems?

Student A: Turn to page 82.
Student B: Turn to page 90.

Speak NOW

1 I learned a lot from...

Student A and Student B: Imagine that you recently experienced one of the big changes listed below. Describe the change to your partner.

You lost your job.

You moved to a new country.

I can ask about significant experiences.
☐ Very well ☐ I need more practice.

I can talk about important events.
☐ Very well ☐ I need more practice.

See Language Booster page 3.

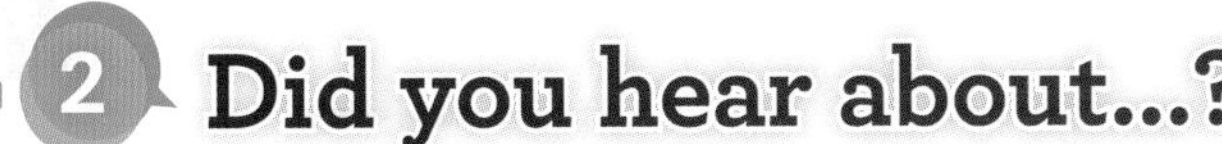

2 Did you hear about...?

Student A and Student B: Take turns introducing and asking for details on the stories below. Use your imagination to make up details of the story.

A man found a box full of gold coins hidden in his basement.

A six-year-old girl wrote a novel.

A dog learned how to tell the time.

I can introduce interesting stories.
☐ Very well ☐ I need more practice.

I can ask for details.
☐ Very well ☐ I need more practice.

See Language Booster page 5.

3 I can't stand it when...

Student A and Student B: Choose one of the pet peeves below. Take turns describing why it bothers you and sympathizing.

People who eat with their mouths open.

People who finish your sentences.

People who are always late to appointments.

I can describe pet peeves.
☐ Very well ☐ I need more practice.

I can sympathize.
☐ Very well ☐ I need more practice.

See Language Booster page 7.

4 You put up with a lot.

Student A and Student B: Choose one of the friendship problems below. Take turns describing a problem and making suggestions.

Your friend is gossiping about you.

Your friend borrowed money from you and won't pay you back.

Your friend said he was busy, but he lied.

I can make suggestions.
☐ Very well ☐ I need more practice.

I can comment on suggestions.
☐ Very well ☐ I need more practice.

See Language Booster page 9.

5 How do you know...?

- Getting to know people
- Asking about people's jobs

1 | Vocabulary

A Imagine that you wanted to invite some people to your home for dinner. Which of these people would you invite? Check (✓) your answers.

____ 1. an **acquaintance** from school

____ 2. an exercise **buddy**

____ 3. an **ex**-boyfriend or -girlfriend

____ 4. a **former** co-worker

____ 5. your **future** sister-in-law

____ 6. an **old** friend

____ 7. an **old** neighbor

____ 8. a **prospective** employer

B PAIR WORK Who did you choose to invite? Explain your answers to your partner.

Example:

A: Would you invite an acquaintance from school to a dinner at your home?

B: Yes, I would. I have a few acquaintances at school that I would like to get to know better.

2 | Conversation

CD1 12 **A Listen. How does Sarah know Eva? What is Luisa's job?**

Luisa: So, how do you know Eva?

Sarah: Well, Eva's my old neighbor. I used to live in the apartment across from hers.

Luisa: Oh, right. I think we've met before.

Sarah: Yes, you look familiar. You used to come over to visit Eva once in a while.

Luisa: That's right. Eva is a former classmate of mine. We had a few classes together in college, and we used to study together a lot.

Sarah: I see. And what do you do now?

Luisa: I work as an assistant in an advertising firm.

Sarah: That sounds interesting. Do you enjoy it?

Luisa: Yes, I do.

B PAIR WORK Practice the conversation.

CD1 13 **C Listen. Write the three extra sentences you hear in the conversation. Practice the new conversation.**

3 | Language Booster

A **Notice the expressions we can use when we're getting to know people and asking them about their jobs.**

Getting to know people	Asking about people's jobs
How do you know (Eva)?	What do you do?
I think we've met before.	How did you get into that line of business?
Haven't we met?	That sounds interesting. Do you enjoy it?
You look familiar.	How did you get interested in (advertising)?

B **PAIR WORK** **Talk with a partner as though you are meeting each other at a social event.**

Example:

A: Hi, I'm Erica.

B: Hi, Erica. I'm Douglas. You look familiar...

4 | Pronunciation Noun stress

CD1 14 **A** **Listen to these phrases. Notice that the nouns in these phrases get more stress than the adjectives.**

1. former **neigh**bor
2. ex-**boy**friend
3. prospective em**ploy**er
4. old **friend**
5. future **sister**-in-law
6. new **co**-worker

B **PAIR WORK** **Take turns asking and answering the question "*How do you know...?*" Use the cues below to answer. Pay attention to noun stress.**

1. Pedro: a new acquaintance
2. Ana: an old co-worker
3. Theo: a former neighbor
4. Karen: an ex-girlfriend
5. John: your future brother-in-law
6. Angie: an old friend

ONLINE PRACTICE

SPEAK *with* CONFIDENCE

A **Write down on a piece of paper the names of four people that you know well and how you know them. Be creative. These people can be your close friends or famous celebrities.**

B **CLASS ACTIVITY** **Walk around the classroom and "meet" your classmates. In each conversation, imagine that you and your classmate are at a party hosted by one of the people above. Ask and answer questions about how you know that person and about what you do for a living.**

How do you know Scarlett Johansson?

Oh, we worked on a movie together.

Really? What do you do?

SOCIALIZING 5

6 Are you up for...?

- Making invitations
- Declining politely

1 | Vocabulary

A **Read the sentences below about things to do on a weekend night. Check the sentences that are true for you.**

_____ 1. On Friday and Saturday nights, I'm usually **up for** going out.

_____ 2. I like to **catch** a movie with my friends once a week or more.

_____ 3. I like to **get a bite to eat** with friends at least once a week.

_____ 4. I'm really busy, but I'll try to **swing by** for a little while.

_____ 5. I like to **try out** new restaurants whenever I can.

_____ 6. I'm usually really **beat** after work or school, so I don't go during the weekdays.

_____ 7. On some nights, I'm just not **in the mood** to go out, so I stay home.

B **PAIR WORK** **Tell your partner what you like to do on weekend nights.**

2 | Conversation

CD1 15 **A** **Listen. Why do Max and Lia decline Bruno's invitations? Where is Bruno going to go for dinner?**

Bruno: Hey, Max. Are you up for going out tonight? I was thinking we could try out the new Italian restaurant on Market Street. _____

Max: I'm not really in the mood to go out, actually. I'm pretty beat. _____

Bruno: Hi, Lia. What do you say we try out the new Italian place?

Lia: I really wish I could, but I have to study for an exam. _____

Bruno: Hey, Paul. Are you in the mood to get a bite to eat tonight?

Paul: Sure! That sounds great! I don't feel like cooking tonight. Hmmm, how about Thai food?

Bruno: Sure, I'll eat anything at this point. _____

B **PAIR WORK** **Practice the conversation. Then find the best places to add the sentences below to the conversation and practice it again.**

1. I've heard that it's great!	3. I worked ten hours today.
2. I am a bit overwhelmed.	4. I'm starving!

3 | Language Booster

A **Notice the different ways we make invitations and decline politely.**

Making invitations	Declining politely
Are you up for (going out tonight)?	I'm not sure I'm up for that tonight.
Are you in the mood to…?	I really wish I could, but I have to (study for an exam).
How about…?	I'm not really in the mood to go out, actually.
What do you say we try out the…?	That sounds really fun, but I'm afraid I have other plans.
Do you feel like…?	
How does…sound?	

B **PAIR WORK** **Invite your partner to do something tonight. Your partner politely declines.**

4 | Listening

CD1 16 **A** **Listen to people making and responding to invitations. What are they inviting people to do? Number the pictures from 1 to 4.**

a

b

c

d

CD1 16 **B** **Listen again. Why does each person decline the invitation?**

1. ______________________
2. ______________________
3. ______________________
4. ______________________

SPEAK *with* CONFIDENCE

A **Write a reason why you might decline each of the invitations below.**

1. try out the new cafe downtown: ______________________
2. take in a play on Friday evening: ______________________
3. catch a movie on Saturday afternoon: ______________________

B **PAIR WORK** **Take turns making and declining invitations to do the things listed above.**

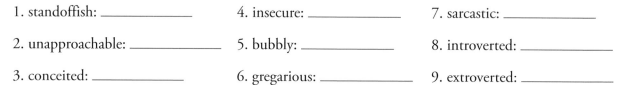

7 I had thought she was...

- Talking about false assumptions
- Summarizing

1 | Vocabulary

A Look at the words and phrases for describing people. Next to each one, write the name of someone you've known in the past who fits the description.

1. standoffish: ________	4. insecure: ________	7. sarcastic: ________
2. unapproachable: ________	5. bubbly: ________	8. introverted: ________
3. conceited: ________	6. gregarious: ________	9. extroverted: ________

B PAIR WORK Describe someone that you know who matches the descriptions above. Explain why you think the person fits that description.

2 | Conversation

CD1 17 **A** Listen. What does Anna think of Susan at the beginning of the conversation? How does she feel at the end?

Anna: Do you know Susan Park?
Crystal: Yeah, I know her. We had a few classes together last semester.

Anna: I don't think she likes me. She seems kind of conceited.

Crystal: Oh, I'm sure she likes you. I used to think she didn't like me, too.
Anna: Really?
Crystal: Yeah. I had thought she was standoffish, but it turns out she is actually just introverted. She's on the quiet side, but she's very witty.

Anna: So what you're saying is you really like her.
Crystal: Yeah, I do. Once she felt comfortable with me, she opened up.

Anna: That's good to know. I'll try a little harder to talk to her.

B PAIR WORK Practice the conversation.

CD1 18 **C** Listen. Write the three extra sentences you hear in the conversation. Practice the new conversation.

3 | Language Booster

A Notice the ways we talk about false assumptions and summarize.

Talking about false assumptions	Summarizing
I had thought she was (standoffish), but it turns out that she is actually just (introverted).	So, what you're saying is (you really like her).
I'd always assumed that she was…, but in reality…	In other words, you didn't really hit it off.
	So, you'd never actually gotten to know her.
Everyone always said she was…, but the truth is she is…	It sounds like everyone had misjudged her.

B **PAIR WORK** Describe someone that you originally made a false assumption about.

Example:

A: My friends have always assumed that I was extroverted, but in reality I'm introverted.

B: It sounds like everyone had misjudged you.

SOCIALIZING 7

4 | Pronunciation Intonation for a change of opinion

CD1 19 **A** Listen to these sentences about false assumptions. Notice the changes in intonation.

1. Everyone always said she was shy, but the truth is she is really gregarious.
2. I'd always assumed that she was conceited, but in reality she's very sweet.

B **PAIR WORK** Take turns making sentences about people using the cues below.

1. rude / polite 2. polite / rude 3. self-confident / insecure 4. insecure / self-confident

ONLINE PRACTICE

SPEAK with CONFIDENCE

A Make a list of three people that you made false assumptions about when you first met them. Write their names, your first assumptions, and what you later learned about them.

Names	First assumptions	What you learned

B **PAIR WORK** Describe the people you listed above to your partner. Your partner summarizes what you say.

8 It's just not my thing.

- Expressing a lack of understanding
- Expressing opinions without offending someone

1 | Vocabulary

A Read the survey below. Write answers to the questions.

1. How do you **keep up with** old friends? ______________________
2. Do you **participate** in social networking? ______________________
3. How often do you **post** messages on people's **walls**? ______________________
4. How often do you **share links** to articles and videos on your wall? ______________________
5. How many people are you **connected** to? ______________________
6. Do you ever **upload** photos and **tag** people in them? ______________________

B PAIR WORK Explain your answers to the survey to your partner.

2 | Conversation

CD1 20 **A Listen. What does Nina like to do on Facebook? Why doesn't Andy spend time on Facebook?**

Nina: Hey, Andy. I posted a message on your wall.

Andy: Oh, sorry. I hardly ever read those messages. _____

Nina: I just don't get why you don't love Facebook. I'm on it all the time.

Andy: It's just not really my thing. _____

Nina: I like to keep up with old friends and connect with new ones. And I like to upload photos of things I do with my friends and family.

Andy: Oh, I don't like it when people tag me in photos.

Nina: Really? I don't see why you don't like to be tagged. _____

Andy: I'm sure it can be fun, but it's just not for me. I'm a pretty private person.

Nina: Yeah, I can understand that. But I also like to check out the links that people share. _____

Andy: I can see why some people like that, but it just doesn't interest me.

B PAIR WORK Practice the conversation. Then find the best places to add the sentences belowto the conversation and practice it again.

1. I don't go on Facebook very often.	3. That's how I get my news.
2. It's fun to see photos of people.	4. What do you do on Facebook?

3 | Language Booster

A Notice the ways we express a lack of understanding and give opinions without offending someone.

Expressing a lack of understanding	Expressing opinions without offending someone
I don't get why you like (Facebook) so much.	I'm sure it can be fun, but it's just not for me.
I guess I don't really understand what you get out of it.	I can see why some people like it, but it just doesn't interest me.
I don't see why you don't like (to be tagged in photos).	It's just not really my thing.
I just don't get why you don't love...	It's not that I don't like..., it's that I like... better.

B **PAIR WORK** Choose a topic below and imagine that your partner likes it, and you don't understand why. Your partner will explain why he or she likes it.

tagging friends | spending time on social networks | commenting on posts | linking with strangers

4 | Listening

CD1 21 **A** Listen to Ben and Dana talk about social networks they like and don't like. Write the name of the person who likes a social network below.

	Name	Reason
Pinterest		
Facebook		
Twitter		

CD1 21 **B** Listen again. Write the reasons why the person likes the social network. Do you use any of the social networks? Do you agree with Dana or Ben?

ONLINE PRACTICE

SPEAK *with* CONFIDENCE

A Make a list of two activities that you really like and two that you really don't like.

Activities you like	Activities you don't like
1.	1.
2.	2.

B **PAIR WORK** Discuss why you like or dislike the activities.

C **GROUP WORK** What's the least popular activity and the most popular activity in the group?

English in Action

ONLINE PRACTICE

SOCIALIZING 5 6 7 8 VIDEO

1 | Preview

PAIR WORK Look at the photos below. What do you think happens? Put them in order from 1 to 4. How do you think Tom and Kate feel in each photo?

2 | Practice

A Watch the video. Answer the questions.

1. Why is Tom going to the cafe?
2. Why doesn't Alex want to go with him?
3. How does Tom know Anna?
4. How does Kate know Anna?
5. Why does Tom look familiar to Kate?
6. What does Tom mean by "small world!"

B Watch the video again. List three things that Tom and Kate have in common.

3 | Discuss

GROUP WORK Answer the questions.

1. Do you like to meet new people? Why or why not?
2. Think of a person you really hit it off with (liked when you first met him/her). Why did you like each other? What did you have in common?
3. Do you have any "small world" stories that have happened to you or someone you know? Share the story.

CONFIDENCE BOOSTER Student A: Turn to page 83.
Student B: Turn to page 91.

Speak NOW

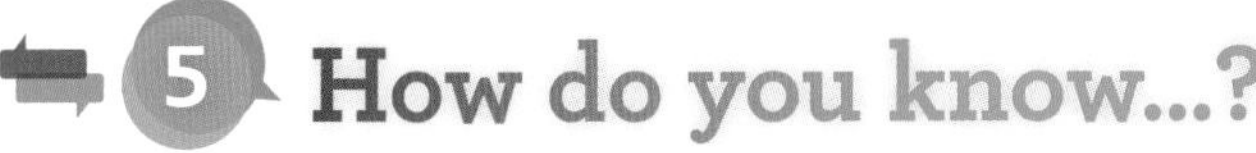

5 How do you know...?

Student A and Student B: Role-play "meeting" and getting to know each other. Use the professions below and your own ideas.

television executive	lawyer
computer animator	guitar player in a band

I can get to know people.
☐ Very well ☐ I need more practice.

I can ask about people's job.
☐ Very well ☐ I need more practice.

See Language Booster page 13.

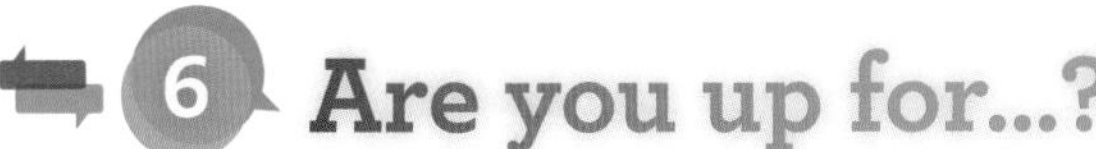

6 Are you up for...?

Student A and Student B: Take turns making and politely declining invitations to do the activities below.

- try out a new raw food restaurant
- get a bite to eat after class
- go to a cafe to listen to your friend's band play

I can make invitations.
☐ Very well ☐ I need more practice.

I can decline invitations politely.
☐ Very well ☐ I need more practice.

See Language Booster page 15.

7 I had thought she was...

Student A and Student B: Take turns talking about false assumptions about people using the descriptions below.

unfriendly / shy	extroverted / introverted	on the quiet side / bubbly
sarcastic / sweet	a homebody / gregarious	rude / warm

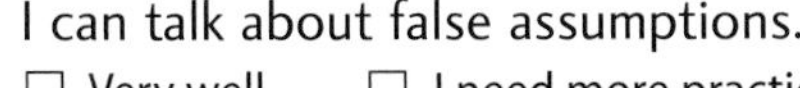

I can talk about false assumptions.
☐ Very well ☐ I need more practice.

I can summarize what someone said.
☐ Very well ☐ I need more practice.

See Language Booster page 17.

8 It's just not my thing.

Student A and Student B: You and your partner each choose two of the activities below. You like the activities that you choose, and your partner doesn't. Discuss why you like or dislike the activities.

connecting through Skype	chatting online
blogging	reading the news online

I can express a lack of understanding.
☐ Very well ☐ I need more practice.

I can express opinions without offending someone.
☐ Very well ☐ I need more practice.

See Language Booster page 19.

9 What exactly is a...?

- Asking for clarification
- Giving clarification

1 | Vocabulary

A Complete the questionnaire below about your eating habits.

	Not at all true	Somewhat true	Very true
1. I eat **junk food** on a regular basis.			
2. I try to have **nutritious** food at every meal.			
3. I have a **vegan** diet.			
4. I'm a **vegetarian**.			
5. I eat only **organic** produce.			
6. I try to eat **locally-sourced** produce whenever I can.			
7. I consider myself a **locavore**.			
8. I eat a lot of **processed foods**.			

B PAIR WORK Explain your answers to the questionnaire to your partner.

2 | Conversation

CD1 22 **A Listen. Where does Julia want to go for lunch? Why doesn't Eric want to go there?**

Julia: Hey, Eric. I'm starving. Do you want to have lunch?

Eric: Yeah, I'm hungry, too.

Julia: Great. How about the burger place downtown?

Eric: Oh, well, I don't really like to eat junk food. And actually, I'm a vegan.

Julia: What do you mean by "vegan"? Is that the same thing as a vegetarian?

Eric: It's not exactly the same thing. A vegan is a person who doesn't eat any animal products, not even milk or cheese.

Julia: Oh, I see. Where would you like to eat?

Eric: I've been wanting to try the new sandwich place. All their food is organic and locally sourced.

Julia: I'm not sure what you mean by "locally sourced."

Eric: What I mean is all the food comes from local farms.

Julia: Oh, well, that sounds great.

B PAIR WORK Practice the conversation.

CD1 23 **C Listen. Write the three extra sentences you hear in the conversation. Practice the new conversation.**

3 | Language Booster

A Notice the different ways we ask for and give clarification.

Asking for clarification	Giving clarification
What do you mean by ("vegan")?	A (vegan) is a person who (doesn't eat any animal products)
What exactly is a…?	It's a…
I don't really get what…means.	It means…
I'm not sure what you mean by…	What I mean is…

B **PAIR WORK** Choose one of the words or phrases below to explain. Look them up in a dictionary if necessary. Then take turns asking and answering for clarification about the words.

artificial ingredients　　dietary restrictions　　gluten-free diet

Example:

A: I can't eat pizza. I have dietary restrictions.

B: What do you mean by "dietary restrictions"?

LIFESTYLES 9

4 | Pronunciation Word stress in a sentence

CD1 24 **A** Listen to the sentences. Notice that the most important words, or the content words, are stressed. Words like articles, prepositions, pronouns, and auxiliary verbs are not stressed.

A: I **don't really get** what **"locally sourced" means.**

B: It **means all** the **food comes** from **local farms.**

B **PAIR WORK** Tell a partner about one of your eating habits or restrictions. Pay attention to the word stress in your sentences.

ONLINE PRACTICE

SPEAK *with* CONFIDENCE

A Write down your own eating habits.

Foods you like to eat:	Foods you don't eat:
__________	__________
__________	__________
Foods you eat frequently:	**Foods you should eat more often:**
__________	__________
__________	__________

B **GROUP WORK** Share information about your eating habits. Ask for and give clarification.

10

I decided to...

- Giving reasons
- Expressing approval

1 | Vocabulary

A Look at the article about keeping a clean home environment. Choose the correct word in each pair to complete the article.

Is **clutter / declutter** in your home affecting your life? Some researchers have found that a messy home can cause people to **tidy up / procrastinate** on their tasks and can make them feel tired all the time. **Tidy up / Procrastinating** your stacks of papers and magazines and **organizing / sticking to** your life may feel like an enormous job, but you can **neat / declutter** your home a little bit at a time. Don't do it all at once, and don't do it **stick to it / at the last minute** before weekend houseguests are due to arrive. Instead, take 15 minutes at the end of each workday to clean up a small area of your home. Make this activity a daily habit and **stick to it / procrastinate**. Say goodbye to clutter for good!

B PAIR WORK Discuss the ideas in the article. Do you think clutter can affect a person's life? Explain.

2 | Conversation

CD1 25 **A Listen. What did Leo do? Why did he do it?**

Michele: Hey, Leo. Your desk is so neat now. _____

Leo: Well, I decided to get organized and tidy up my work station because I can never find anything.

Michele: That's great! And is that a calendar on your computer screen? _____

Leo: Yes, it is. I'm always procrastinating and doing things at the last minute, so I decided to make a schedule for myself and stick to it. _____

Michele: I'm impressed. And how is it all working out for you? Are you getting more done?

Leo: Not really. I'm actually behind in my work because I've spent the last two days getting organized. And I think my desk is too neat now! _____

B PAIR WORK Practice the conversation. Then find the best places to add the sentences below to the conversation and practice it again.

1. I can't find anything.	3. I've never seen you use a calendar before.
2. What happened?	4. It will also help me be on time for meetings.

3 | Language Booster

A Notice the ways we give reasons and express approval.

Giving reasons	Expressing approval
I decided to (get organized) because (I can never find anything).	Good for you!
I'm always…, so I decided to…	That's great!
Since I…, I decided to…	I'm impressed

B **PAIR WORK** Tell your partner about one thing you'd like to change about yourself and why.

Example:

A: Since I can never remember important appointments, I decided to organize my calendar.

B: That's great!

4 | Listening

CD1 26 **A** Listen. Sandra is organizing her room. Number the topics in the order that you hear them.

Topics	Reasons for the changes
_____ try on clothes	
_____ get rid of some clothes and books	
_____ neaten up closet	
_____ make room on bookshelf	
_____ organize desk	

CD1 26 **B** Listen again. Write the reason for each change in the chart above.

ONLINE PRACTICE

SPEAK with CONFIDENCE

A Make a list of some ways that you can organize your life better and the problems that this organization might help with.

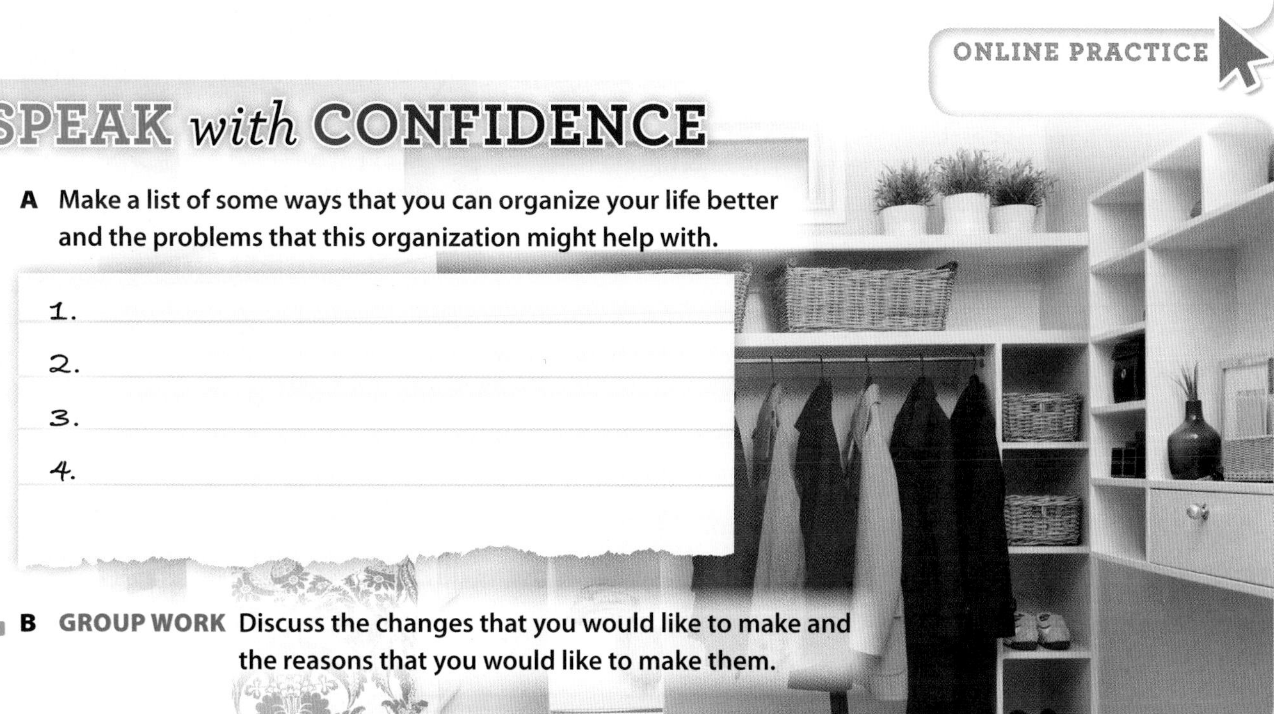

1.
2.
3.
4.

B **GROUP WORK** Discuss the changes that you would like to make and the reasons that you would like to make them.

11 I spend too much time...

- Talking about lifestyles
- Evaluating lifestyle

1 | Vocabulary

A Check the activities below that you do regularly.

_____ 1. reading **blogs**

_____ 2. uploading videos to **video-sharing sites**

_____ 3. watching **live streams** of lectures

_____ 4. downloading smartphone **apps**

_____ 5. visiting **social networking sites**

_____ 6. listening to **podcasts**

_____ 7. communicating with **video chats**

_____ 8. posting messages on **message boards**

B PAIR WORK Tell your partner about two of the activities that you do and how often you do them.

2 | Conversation

CD1 27 **A Listen. Why does Michael look so tired? What does Michael decide that he needs to do?**

David: You look tired, Michael.

Michael: Yeah, I spent the whole night updating my website and posting on message boards.

David: Weren't you up really late the night before, too?

Michael: Uh-huh. I was up half the night watching a live stream of a concert.

David: You didn't sleep much over the weekend either.

Michael: I know. I was busy researching and writing new blog posts. I was also uploading videos to a video-sharing site.

David: I'm surprised that you can even talk to me right now.

Michael: I know. I should really get more sleep. I spend too much time online.

B PAIR WORK Practice the conversation.

CD1 28 **C Listen. Write the three extra sentences you hear in the conversation. Practice the new conversation.**

3 | Language Booster

A Notice the ways we talk about and evaluate lifestyles.

Talking about lifestyles		Evaluating lifestyles
I was up half the night I spent the whole night	updating my website.	I spend too much time (online). I should really (get more sleep). I need to limit…
I was out most of the day…		

B PAIR WORK Look at the technology-related lifestyle habits below. Which ones apply to you? Discuss and evaluate your lifestyles.

watching TV until late at night	eating junk food
spending a lot of money shopping online	checking for texts every five minutes

LIFESTYLES 11

4 | Pronunciation Reduction of *-ing* endings

CD1 29 **A** Listen to the sentences. Notice the reduction of *-ing* endings which makes the *-ing* sound like *in'*.

1. I was up all night **updatin' my website.**
2. I spent the whole night **watchin'** videos.
3. I spend too much time **chattin'** online.
4. I was out most of the day **runnin'** errands.

B PAIR WORK Think of a recent day when you were busy. Tell a partner what you spent most of the day doing. Pay attention to reducing *-ing* endings.

ONLINE PRACTICE

SPEAK *with* CONFIDENCE

A Write three technology-related activities that you did in the last week that you feel are bad lifestyle habits.

1. ______________________________
2. ______________________________
3. ______________________________

B GROUP WORK Discuss the lifestyle habits that you wrote above.

C CLASS ACTIVITY Share your group lifestyle habits. What are some common lifestyle habits?

12 You have a point, but...

- Persuading
- Disagreeing politely

1 | Vocabulary

A Look at the words and phrases below. Write each one in the correct category in the chart.

energy-efficient appliances
global warming
greenhouse gases
recycling
waste
public transportation
landfill
hybrid cars
reducing your carbon footprint

Things that hurt the environment	Things that can improve the environment

B PAIR WORK Discuss things you do to protect the environment.

2 | Conversation

CD1 30 **A** Listen. Why does Mia use CFL bulbs? Why doesn't Paula want to use them?

Paula: Is that one of those CFL bulbs? What are they?
Mia: Yeah, it is. CFL stands for compact fluorescent light bulbs. I only use these now. ____
Paula: But aren't those light bulbs kind of expensive? ____

Mia: Sure, they're a little more expensive, but they last a lot longer than incandescent bulbs. And they're better for the environment because they're energy-efficient. ____
Paula: You have a point, but it's still costly. ____

Mia: But don't you think we should do whatever we can to reduce our carbon footprints?
Paula: Yes, I guess we should, but I'm still not convinced that CFL bulbs are the most environmentally responsible choice.

B PAIR WORK Practice the conversation. Then find the best places to add the sentences below to the conversation and practice it again.

1. They use about a third of the energy that regular bulbs use.
2. I heard that they cost a lot.
3. I really like them.
4. I'm trying to save money.

3 | Language Booster

A **Notice the ways we persuade and disagree politely.**

Persuading	Disagreeing politely
Don't you think (we should do whatever we can)?	You have a point, but (it's still costly).
Isn't it important to…?	I see what you mean, but…
If everyone…, then…	That may be true, but on the other hand…
	I guess…, but I'm still not convinced…

B **PAIR WORK** **Consider the ideas you discussed in the Vocabulary section. Describe one way to protect the environment and persuade your partner that it is important.**

4 | Listening

CD1 31 **A** **Listen to three conversations about environmental topics. Number the pictures from 1 to 3. There is one extra.**

a  ☐

b  ☐

c  ☐

d  ☐

CD1 31 **B** **Listen again. Do the speakers successfully persuade the people that they're talking to? Write** ***yes*** **or** ***no*****.**

1. ______________ 2. ______________ 3. ______________

ONLINE PRACTICE

SPEAK *with* CONFIDENCE

A **PAIR WORK** **Write one thing that you both think people should do to protect the environment and brainstorm as many persuasive arguments as you can.**

Way to protect the environment:

____

____

Persuasive arguments:

____

____

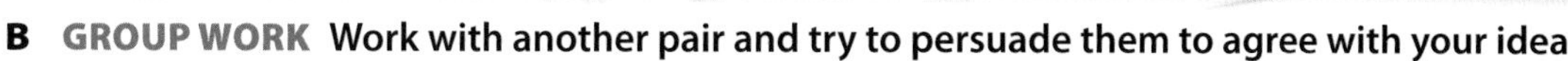

B **GROUP WORK** **Work with another pair and try to persuade them to agree with your idea.**

English in Action

ONLINE PRACTICE

1 | Preview

PAIR WORK **Look at the photos. What kind of changes do you think Maria is making to her lifestyle? Why?**

a

b

LIFESTYLES

9

10

11

12

VIDEO

2 | Practice

A **Read the story below. Then watch the video and cross out the incorrect information.**

Maria slept past noon on Saturday because she'd been up half the night ~~updating her blog.~~ Maria explained to Kate that she intended to make some changes to her lifestyle in order to save money. She planned to turn off the lights during the day, use flashlights instead of electric lights, and do more recycling.

Kate told Maria that she was trying to be more productive because she'd been very lazy lately. She was getting many things done at once: organizing papers, listening to music, chatting on the phone, doing laundry, and learning Chinese.

That afternoon, Tom and Maria got together at a park. Maria complained to Tom that her roommate was sarcastic and loud. Then Tom told Maria about an interesting woman named Kate that he'd met recently. When they realized that Tom's new friend was the same person as Maria's roommate, they had a good laugh.

B **Watch the video again. Correct the mistakes in the story above.**

3 | Discuss

GROUP WORK **Answer the questions.**

1. Who would you rather have as a roommate, Maria or Kate? Why?
2. What qualities do you think are important in a good roommate?
3. Do you sometimes do several things at the same time? Which things?

CONFIDENCE BOOSTER Student A: Turn to page 84.
Student B: Turn to page 92.

9 What exactly is a...?

Student A and Student B: Choose one of the dietary restrictions below or think of your own. Ask for and give clarification as necessary.

dairy-free diet | nut-free diet | carb-free diet

I can ask for clarification.
☐ Very well ☐ I need more practice.

I can give clarification.
☐ Very well ☐ I need more practice.

See Language Booster page 23.

10 I decided to...

Student A and Student B: Choose two of the actions below and imagine reasons why you would want to do them. Then explain the changes and why you are making them.

You decided to reorganize your home.
You decided to get a complete makeover.
You decided to move to another country.

I can give reasons.
☐ Very well ☐ I need more practice.

I can express approval.
☐ Very well ☐ I need more practice.

See Language Booster page 25.

11 I spend too much time...

Student A and Student B: Choose one of these lifestyle habits and come up with your own. Then discuss and evaluate the habit with your partner.

I spend a lot of time shopping. | I play a lot of online games.
I stay up too late reading. | I watch sports a lot.

I can talk about lifestyles.
☐ Very well ☐ I need more practice.

I can evaluate lifestyles.
☐ Very well ☐ I need more practice.

See Language Booster page 27.

12 You have a point, but...

Student A and Student B: Choose one of the actions below or think of your own. Persuade your partner to do it while he or she disagrees politely.

Ride a bike to school or work. | Stop eating meat.

I can persuade someone.
☐ Very well ☐ I need more practice.

I can disagree politely.
☐ Very well ☐ I need more practice.

See Language Booster page 29.

LIFESTYLES 9 10 11 12 REVIEW

13 My short-term goal is...

- Asking about career ambitions
- Talking about career ambitions

1 | Vocabulary

A Look at the letter to a career counselor. Complete the sentences with the words in the box.

a. career path	c. entry-level job	e. position	g. raise
b. dream job	d. long-term	f. promotion	h. short-term

Seeking career advice

Dear Ms. Marcus:

Currently, I work as a receptionist in a law firm. It's a(n) ____________, but I'm learning a lot about the law. Next week, I'm going to interview for a ____________ as a research assistant. That job comes with a 40% _____ in salary! Also, I can get a ____________ to lead research assistant after a couple of years. However, that's only my ____________ goal. My ____________ goal is to go to law school. My ____________ is to work as an attorney for a professional sports team! The problem is that I'm not sure if I'm on the correct ____________. How can I get into sports law, specifically? Can you help me?

B PAIR WORK Take turns describing your long-term and short-term goals.

2 | Conversation

CD1 32 **A Listen. What kind of job is Juliana going to interview for? What does Dan want to be?**

Juliana: I have an interview tomorrow. I'm a little nervous.

Dan: What kind of job are you hoping to get?

Juliana: Well, I'm interviewing for the position of production assistant, but my long-term goal is to become a film director.

Dan: Wow, that's exciting. I didn't know you wanted to work in the movies.

Juliana: How about you?

Dan: I hope to get a job working with people. I'd like to work in the medical field. I want to be a nurse.

Juliana: You would be a great nurse!

Dan: Thank you! Good luck on your interview tomorrow!

B PAIR WORK Practice the conversation.

CD1 33 **C Listen. Write the three extra sentences you hear in the conversation. Practice the new conversation.**

pair with VOCABULARY WORKSHEET 1

3 | Language Booster

A **Notice the different ways we ask and talk about career ambitions.**

Asking about career ambitions	Talking about career ambitions
What are your career plans?	My long-term goal is to (become a film director).
What field would you like to get into?	I'd like to work in the (medical) field.
What kind of job are you hoping to get?	My short-term goal is to…
What's your dream job?	I hope to get a job…

B **PAIR WORK** **Ask and answer questions about your career goals using your own ideas.**

Examples:

A: What field would you like to get into?

B: I'd like to work in the education field. What kind of job are you hoping to get?

4 | Pronunciation Adjective Stress

CD1 34 **A** **Listen and practice. Notice how in these compound nouns, the adjective is stressed rather than the noun.**

1. **dream** job
2. **entry-level** job
3. **part-time** job
4. **short-term** goal
5. **long-term** goal
6. **graduate** school

B **GROUP WORK** **Take turns asking and answering the questions below. Pay attention to adjective stress in the compound nouns.**

1. Would you take a job even if it's not your part of your long-term goal?
2. Would you take an entry-level job in the field that you're interested in?

ONLINE PRACTICE

SPEAK *with* CONFIDENCE

A **PAIR WORK** **Complete the information below. Then ask and answer questions about your dream jobs, and your short- and long-term goals for getting your dream jobs.**

Dream job:	
Short–term goals	Long-term goals

What field would you like to get into?

My short-term goal is to get a job at a bakery. My long-term goal is to open my own bakery.

B **GROUP WORK** **Join another pair and describe your partner's career plans.**

14 I'm very organized.

- Asking interview questions
- Describing strengths and weaknesses

1 | Vocabulary

A What kind of person are you in a work environment? Check (✓) the words that describe you.

_____ detail oriented	_____ a hard worker	_____ a team player
_____ efficient	_____ a self-starter	_____ professional
_____ organized	_____ a perfectionist	_____ motivated

B PAIR WORK Take turns describing yourselves. Use the words above.

Examples:

A: How would you describe yourself?

B: I'm very detail oriented. I pay attention to small things.

2 | Conversation

CD1 35 **A Listen. What are Kyle's strengths and weaknesses? Do you think he will get the job?**

Olivia: All right, Kyle. Now I'd like to ask, what would you bring to our organization? _____

Kyle: Well, I'm very organized. I can keep track of a lot of different tasks at a time.

Olivia: I see. _____

Kyle: Also, I'm extremely efficient. _____

Olivia: That's excellent. And what is your biggest weakness?

Kyle: Let me think. Sometimes I'm too detail-oriented, but that can be useful when I'm writing a report.

Olivia: And what is the biggest challenge you've ever faced at work?

Kyle: Good question. Well, once I had to work with a team of 30 people. _____ That was difficult, but I'm a good team player.

B PAIR WORK Practice the conversation. Then find the best places to add the sentences below to the conversation and practice it again.

1. We had to complete a big project in a week.	3. In other words, what are your greatest strengths?
2. We need someone who is organized.	4. I can do a lot of work in a short amount of time.

3 | Language Booster

A Notice the way we ask interview questions and describe strengths and weaknesses.

Asking interview questions	Describing strengths and weaknesses
What would you bring to our organization? What are your greatest strengths?	Well, I'm very (organized). Let's see. I'm a (hard worker). I have good (writing) skills.
What is your biggest weakness?	Sometimes I'm too (detail oriented). I used to/didn't use to..., but now I....
What is the biggest challenge you've ever faced at work?	Let me think. Once I had to...

*Use the the expressions "*That's an interesting question.*" and "*Good question.*" for difficult questions.

B PAIR WORK Take turns asking and answering interview questions about strengths and weaknesses.

4 | Listening

CD1 36 **A Listen. Check (✓) the correct interviewee for each strength and weakness.**

	Lina	Gil
cooperative		
detail oriented		
good people skills		
organized		

	Lina	Gil
a perfectionist		
a professional		
responsible		
a self-starter		

CD1 36 **B Listen again. What were Lina's and Gil's biggest challenges at work?**

Lina: ______________________ Gil: ______________________

ONLINE PRACTICE

SPEAK *with* CONFIDENCE

A Complete the chart with your strengths, weaknesses, and biggest work-related challenges.

Greatest strengths	Biggest weaknesses	Biggest challenges
	I used to / didn't use to ______________________, but now I ______________________. Sometimes I ______________________, but that can be useful when ______________________.	

B PAIR WORK Take turns interviewing each other.

15 The first thing you need...

- Giving clear instructions
- Restating to show that you understand

1 | Vocabulary

A Complete the sentences with the words in the box.

a. bar code	c. code	e. ring up	g. touchscreen
b. cash drawer	d. discount	f. scan	h. transaction

1. A salesperson uses the ____ to enter a private number called the ____.
2. A salesperson will ____ the tag that has a specific ____ to ____ the item.
3. Usually the ____ will open if you are paying in cash.
4. Before you complete your ____, the salesperson will tell you if there is a ____ on the item.

B PAIR WORK Quiz your partner on four of the new words.

2 | Conversation

CD1 37 **A Listen. What is the first step to completing a sales transaction? What is the last step?**

Pam: I want to show you how to complete a sales transaction. The first thing you need to do is enter your employee code on the touchscreen. Then scan the bar code on the first item to ring it up.

Ben: Yes, that makes sense. I need to make sure I don't scan it twice. Or I'll ring it up twice.

Pam: Exactly. The next step is to make sure that the customer gets the correct discount if the item is on sale.

Ben: I see. So I have to check the discount list, right?

Pam: Yes, that's right. After you've checked on the discounts, you hit the "total" key. The total amount will appear at the top of the register.

B PAIR WORK Practice the conversation.

CD1 38 **C Listen. Write the three extra sentences you hear in the conversation. Practice the new conversation.**

3 | Language Booster

A **Notice the ways we give clear instructions and show that we understand.**

Giving clear instructions	Restating to show that you understand
The first thing you need to do is (enter your employee code).	Yes, that makes sense. I need to (make sure I don't scan it twice).
The next step is to…	I see. So I have to…, right?
After you've…, you…	So you're saying that…
It's important to…	So what you're saying is that…
Keep in mind that…	

B **PAIR WORK** **Describe two steps and one important point in a process that you are familiar with. Choose from the topics below or choose your own topic.**

cooking your favorite meal | using your smartphone to send e-mails | completing a household chore

CAREERS

15

4 | Pronunciation Intonation in clarifying questions

CD1 39 **A** **Listen to these clarifying questions. Notice the rising intonation at the ends of the sentences.**

1. I see. So I have to turn the power on first, right?
2. So you're saying that I turn on the alarm before I lock the front door?

B **PAIR WORK** **Take turns explaining the steps in one of the processes in the Language Booster section, part B above. Your partner will restate what you said.**

ONLINE PRACTICE

SPEAK *with* CONFIDENCE

A **Think of a process that you are very familiar with. Write down at least four steps, including a final step, and one thing that it is important to keep in mind.**

1. ______________________
2. ______________________
3. ______________________
4. ______________________

Important thing to keep in mind:

____

B **PAIR WORK** **Take turns describing the process you outlined. Your partner restates what you said to show he or she understood.**

16 I'm here to talk about...

- Giving presentations
- Asking follow-up questions

1 | Vocabulary

A Check (✓) the things that you <u>should</u> do before, during, and after a job interview.

Before the interview		During and after the Interview	
rehearse with a friend		be positive	
research the company		talk about what you don't like to do	
prepare a list of questions		make **eye contact**	
send your **resume**		**stay calm**	
be punctual		**say negative things**	
dress professionally		write a **thank you note**	

B PAIR WORK Explain your answers to your partner.

2 | Conversation

CD1 40 **A** Listen. What is the speaker giving a presentation about? What is one tip that the speaker offers?

Speaker: I'm here to talk about how to have a successful interview. First, I want to talk about how to prepare. Before you go to your interview, research the company to learn about the company's goals and policies. You should also rehearse with a friend. ______

Speaker: Next, let's explore ways to make a good first impression. It's very important to be punctual. If you're late for your interview, your prospective employer may think that you're irresponsible. It's also important to be positive. ______

Speaker: Does anyone have any questions? ______

Student: Yes, at the beginning of your presentation, you said we should research the company. Should we prepare a list of questions to ask? ______

Speaker: Yes, that is definitely a good idea.

B PAIR WORK Practice the conversation. Then find the best places to add the sentences below to the conversation and practice it again.

1. No one wants to hire a person with a bad attitude.
2. That way you won't be nervous.
3. Yes, you in the front row.
4. Is that OK to do?

3 | Language Booster

A **Notice the ways we give presentations and ask follow-up questions.**

Giving presentations	Asking follow-up questions
Today, I'm going to talk about…	
I'm here to talk about…	Could you say more about…?
First, I want to talk about…	You mentioned… Could you explain that further?
Next, let's explore…	At the beginning of your presentation, you said…
To conclude/wrap up…	Could you say more about/give more examples of…
Does anyone have any questions?	

B **PAIR WORK** **Take turns giving the beginning of a presentation and asking follow-up questions.**

Examples:

A: Today, I'm going to talk about good ways to look for a job. First, I want to talk about networking. A lot of people find jobs through people they know…

B: You mentioned networking. Could you explain that further?

4 | Listening

CD1 41 **A** **Listen to someone giving a presentation. What is he talking about? Check the correct topic.**

____ 1. How to talk to your boss about your achievements at work

____ 2. How to get along better with your co-workers and your supervisor

____ 3. How to ask for more money or more responsibility at work

CD1 41 **B** **Listen again. Write down four of the tips he offers.**

1. ____________________ 3. ____________________

2. ____________________ 4. ____________________

ONLINE PRACTICE

SPEAK *with* CONFIDENCE

A **Think of a topic that you know a lot about. Complete the chart below about the topic.**

Topic:
Point 1:
Point 2:
Concluding idea:

Today I am going to talk about shopping on a budget.

B **GROUP WORK** **Take turns giving presentations to your group and asking and answering follow-up questions.**

English in Action

ONLINE PRACTICE

1 | Preview

PAIR WORK **Alex is practicing a presentation that he's going to give at work. What advice do you think Maria and Tom give him? Check (✓) your guesses.**

____ 1. Speak more slowly.

____ 2. Speak more quickly.

____ 3. Say more about your achievements.

____ 4. Make eye contact.

____ 5. Say more about your problems.

____ 6. Don't say "um."

____ 7. Use a smaller font on your slides.

____ 8. Memorize your presentation.

CAREERS

13

14

15

16

VIDEO

2 | Practice

A **Watch the video. What advice did Maria and Tom give Alex? Did you guess correctly?**

B **Watch the video again. Complete the sentences.**

1. Tom is happy because ________________.
2. Alex is nervous because ________________.
3. Alex doesn't like his boss because ________________.
4. Maria is discouraged because ________________.
5. After watching Alex practice his presentation for three hours, Maria and Tom are ________________.

3 | Discuss

GROUP WORK **Answer the questions.**

1. How do you feel when you speak in front of people? Is it easier to speak in front of a small group or a large group? Why?
2. Think of a time when you gave a presentation. What did you do well? What did you need to improve?
3. Think of a person (someone you know or a famous person) who is a good public speaker. What makes him or her a good speaker?

CONFIDENCE BOOSTER Student A: Turn to page 85.
Student B: Turn to page 93.

Speak NOW

13 My short-term goal is...

Student A and Student B: Take turns describing the career paths for the jobs below. Include your short-term goals to get the job.

movie director	race car driver
successful novelist	TV talk show host

I can ask about career ambitions.
☐ Very well ☐ I need more practice.

I can talk about career ambitions.
☐ Very well ☐ I need more practice.

See Language Booster page 33.

14 I'm very organized.

Student A and Student B: You are both interviewing for the same jobs below. Take turns interviewing for the jobs. Describe your strengths and weaknesses.

video game creator	executive of an advertising company
fashion designer	journalist

I can ask interview questions.
☐ Very well ☐ I need more practice.

I can describe my strengths and weaknesses.
☐ Very well ☐ I need more practice.

See Language Booster page 35.

15 The first thing you need...

Student A and Student B: Take turns giving clear instructions for the processes below. Your partner restates to show that he or she understands.

a process you learned at a job	completing your least favorite household chore

I can give clear instructions.
☐ Very well ☐ I need more practice.

I can restate to show that I understand.
☐ Very well ☐ I need more practice.

See Language Booster page 37.

16 I'm here to talk about...

Student A and Student B: Take turns giving short presentation on one of the topics below, or choose your own topic. Ask follow-up questions.

- two interesting blogs or books
- the two best restaurants in your neighborhood
- two of your favorite TV shows

I can give presentations.
☐ Very well ☐ I need more practice.

I can ask follow-up questions.
☐ Very well ☐ I need more practice.

See Language Booster page 39.

ONLINE PRACTICE

17 Are you afraid of...?

- Asking about fears
- Talking about fears

1 | Vocabulary

A Complete the questionnaire about fears. Check (✓) the correct column or columns for each type of fear.

Do you or does someone you know have any of these fears?	You	Someone you know
1. fear of heights		
2. fear of public speaking		
3. fear of flying		
4. fear of the dark		
5. fear of spiders		
6. fear of snakes		
7. claustrophobia		

B **PAIR WORK** Compare your chart with a partner's chart. Do you have any of the same fears? What is the most common fear? What is the least common fear?

2 | Conversation

CD2 02 **A** Listen. What is Daniel afraid of? What is Anthony afraid of?

Daniel: I'm really nervous. I have to give a presentation tomorrow.

Anthony: Oh, you don't like public speaking?

Daniel: That's an understatement. I'm terrified of it!

Anthony: Yeah, a lot of people are. In fact, I've heard that it's one of the most common fears.

Daniel: Really?

Anthony: Yeah. It's even more common than the fear of flying.

Daniel: Are you afraid of public speaking?

Anthony: No, not really.

Daniel: What are you afraid of?

Anthony: Well, I have claustrophobia. I'm afraid of being in small spaces. I'm also uncomfortable around snakes and spiders. They give me the creeps.

B **PAIR WORK** Practice the conversation.

CD2 03 **C** Listen. Write the three extra sentences you hear in the conversation. Practice the new conversation.

pair with VOCABULARY WORKSHEET 17

3 | Language Booster

A **Notice the ways we ask about and talk about fears.**

Asking about fears	Talking about fears
What are you afraid of?	I'm afraid of/scared of/terrified of (public speaking).
Are you afraid of (public speaking)?	I'm nervous (about public speaking).
What's your greatest fear?	(Public speaking) makes me nervous.
Do (snakes and spiders) scare you?	I'm uncomfortable around (snakes and spiders). (They) give me the creeps.

B **PAIR WORK** **Ask and tell your partner about one of your fears.**

Examples:

A: What's your greatest fear?

B: I'm scared of spiders. They make me nervous.

FEELINGS 17

4 | Pronunciation Using a low tone to show negative emotion

CD2 04 **A** **Listen to these sentences. Notice the low tone used for the words that show negative or serious emotion. Compare it with the higher tone used for positive emotion.**

Negative	Positive
1. What's your greatest fear?	What's your favorite color?
2. I'm afraid of flying.	I really like flying.
3. Snakes give me the creeps.	Snakes are fascinating creatures.

B **PAIR WORK** **Ask and tell your partner about one fear, like you did in the Language Booster section, part B above. This time, be sure to use a low tone for negative words.**

ONLINE PRACTICE

SPEAK *with* CONFIDENCE

A **PAIR WORK** **List things that you are afraid of below and discuss them with your partner.**

Fears:

B **GROUP WORK** **Talk about the fears you listed above. What are some common fears?**

18 I'm overworked.

- Talking about causes of stress
- Giving advice by talking about personal experiences

1 | Vocabulary

A **Match the causes of stress on the left with the ways to manage stress on the right.**

____ 1. too many **deadlines**	a. try some **relaxation techniques**
____ 2. a **misunderstanding** with a friend	b. try **meditating**
____ 3. **overworked**	c. **drop** a class
____ 4. under too much **pressure**	d. **talk through** your problems
____ 5. really **stressed**	e. talk to your boss about your **workload**

B **PAIR WORK** **Discuss your answers and other possible ways to manage these causes of stress.**

2 | Conversation

CD2 05 **A** **Listen. Why are Walker and Julia stressed? What advice does Julia give Walker?**

Julia: Hi, Walker. Are you OK? ____

Walker: Oh, hi, Julia. I am stressed. I have too many deadlines.

Julia: How many classes are you taking? ____

Walker: I'm taking six classes.

Julia: In my experience, six is too many classes. I've found that it's helpful to drop a class and take it the following semester.

Walker: You're right. How are you doing? ____

Julia: I'm overworked. I had to work three 12-hour shifts in a row.

Walker: Wow, that's a lot! ____

B **PAIR WORK** **Practice the conversation. Then find the best places to add the sentences below to the conversation and practice it again.**

1. You should talk to your boss!	3. You look a little stressed, too.
2. Are you taking more than five?	4. You look really stressed.

3 | Language Booster

A **Notice the ways we talk about causes of stress and give advice by talking about personal experiences.**

Talking about causes of stress	Giving advice by talking about personal experiences
I have too many deadlines.	I've found that it's really helpful to (drop a class).
I'm overworked.	In my experience (six is too many classes).
I'm under a lot of pressure.	… has always worked well for me.
I'm having problems with a friend.	I always feel better after I…

B **PAIR WORK** **Share one cause of stress with a partner. Your partner will give you advice by talking about his or her own experience.**

Examples:

A: I'm under a lot of pressure at work. My boss expects a lot from me, so I come in early and stay late.

B: That's too bad. In my experience, when people always come in early and stay late, their bosses expect them to do that all the time. What has worked well for me is talking to my boss and telling her…

FEELINGS 18

4 | Listening

CD2 06 **A** **Listen to people talking about stress. Number the causes of stress in the order that you hear them. There is one extra.**

____ a. a co-worker ____ b. problems at home ____ c. a friend ____ d. family problems

CD2 06 **B** **Listen again. Summarize the advice that each person gives.**

1. ____________ 2. ____________ 3. ____________

ONLINE PRACTICE

SPEAK *with* CONFIDENCE

A **PAIR WORK** **Write down two causes of stress in your life. Share your answers with a partner. Your partner will think of his or her own personal experiences that are related to your problems.**

1. ____________ 2. ____________

B **PAIR WORK** **Talk with your partner about your causes of stress. Your partner will give you advice based on his or her own experiences.**

19 If I could go anywhere...

- Talking about dreams and wishes
- Expressing interest and asking for reasons

1 | Vocabulary

A Use the words on the left to complete the phrases on the right.

If I could do anything, I would...

create
discover
develop
establish
explore
revolutionize
invent

1. ______________ a colony on the moon.
2. ______________ a new species of animal
3. ______________ an art program for children in my city
4. ______________ flying shoes
5. ______________ public transportation
6. ______________ the jungles in South America
7. ______________ a beautiful piece of art

B PAIR WORK Take turns asking and answering the question, *"If you could do anything, what would you do?"*

2 | Conversation

CD2 07 **A Listen. What is Alex's dream? What is Sandra's dream?**

Alex: I'm so tired. We've had so many customers today! I think everyone in town is shopping today.
Sandra: I know! I could use a vacation.

Alex: Where would you go if you could go anywhere?
Sandra: If I could go anywhere, I would go to the Bahamas.

Alex: Interesting. Why the Bahamas?
Sandra: First of all, it's beautiful there. Second, I could explore underwater caves.

Alex: That sounds really fun. But I don't really feel like I need a vacation. I think I need a different job.

Sandra: What kind of job do you want?
Alex: If I could have any job, I would be a scientist.
Sandra: Oh, really? Why is that?
Alex: I would love to discover cures for diseases.

Sandra: That sounds great.

B PAIR WORK Practice the conversation.

CD2 08 **C Listen. Write the three extra sentences you hear in the conversation. Practice the new conversation.**

3 | Language Booster

A Notice the ways we talk about dreams and wishes and express interest and ask for reasons.

Talking about dreams and wishes	Expressing interest and asking for reasons
If I could go anywhere, I'd travel to (the Bahamas).	Interesting. Why (the Bahamas)?
If I could do anything, I'd (be a scientist).	
If I could have any job, I would (be a scientist).	Oh, really? Why is that?
If I could meet anyone, I'd meet…	Oh, is that right? How come?

B **PAIR WORK** Tell a partner about one of your dreams or wishes. Use the words from the Vocabulary section or your own ideas.

Examples:

A: If I could do anything, I would go skydiving.

B: Oh, is that right? How come?

FEELINGS

19

4 | Pronunciation Using a high tone to show positive emotion

CD2 09 **A** Listen to these sentences. Notice the high tone used for the words that show positive emotion.

1. If I could go **anywhere**, I would go into space.
2. If I could do **anything,** I would be the leader of the country for one week.
3. If I could meet **anyone**, I would meet my favorite actor.
4. If I could have **any job**, I would be a singer.

B **PAIR WORK** Talk with a partner about a dream or wish you have . This time, be sure to use a high tone when necessary.

ONLINE PRACTICE

SPEAK *with* CONFIDENCE

A **PAIR WORK** Look at the quotes about dreams and wishes from some famous people below. What do you think the quotes mean? Do you agree or disagree?

"Without leaps of imagination, or dreaming, we lose the excitement of possibilities. Dreaming, after all, is a form of planning." –*Gloria Steinem*

"There is nothing like a dream to create the future." –*Victor Hugo*

B **GROUP WORK** Talk about your own dreams and wishes.

20 I wish I had...

- Asking about regrets
- Talking about regrets

1 | Vocabulary

A Look at the questions below. Check the appropriate column.

When you were a child did you...	Yes	No	Sometimes
1. **goof off** in school?			
2. get involved in a **clique**?			
3. try hard to **fit in**?			
4. **pick on** other kids?			
5. **give** your parents **a hard time**?			
6. **take** school **seriously**?			
7. have an **active social life**?			
8. **get involved in** activities?			

B PAIR WORK Take turns sharing your answers to the questions in the chart.

2 | Conversation

CD2 10 **A Listen. What does Nina regret? What would she do differently?**

Paul: Are you taking a math class this semester, Nina? _____

Nina: Yeah, I am. I took math in high school, but I didn't do well because I was always goofing around. I wish I had taken school more seriously. _____

Paul: What else do you wish you had done when you were young?

Nina: I wish I hadn't gotten involved in a clique. Those friends were a bad influence on me. If only I had had nicer friends, I might have been a better student. _____

Paul: Well, we all learn from our mistakes.

Nina: You're right. _____

B PAIR WORK Practice the conversation. Then find the best places to add the sentences below to the conversation and practice it again.

1. Then maybe I wouldn't be having such a hard time now.
2. That looks like a math book.
3. I've learned a few things since high school.
4. It's hard making good friends in high school.

3 | Language Booster

A Notice the ways we ask about and talk about regrets.

Asking about regrets	Talking about regrets
If you could do it over, what would you do differently?	I wish I'd (taken school more seriously).
What / Where / Who / When — do you wish you…?	I wish I hadn't (gotten involved in a clique).
Do you wish you had…?	I regret…
	I (never) should have…
	If only I had/hadn't…
	If I could do it over, I would…

B **PAIR WORK** Talk with a partner about one regret that you have from your early teen years and what you would do differently if you could.

4 | Listening

CD2 11 **A** Listen to Jack and Clara talk about regrets. Check (✓)the regrets that you hear.

☐ 1. not going with Jack	☐ 6. going to South Beach
☐ 2. taking a vacation	☐ 7. going on vacation with friends
☐ 3. listening to brother's advice	☐ 8. coming home on Sunday
☐ 4. staying in the hotel from last year	☐ 9. taking an early morning class
☐ 5. buying a new computer	☐ 10. swimming in a lake

CD2 11 **B** Listen again. Where did the speakers go? Where would they go if they could do it again?

1. Clara went to ______________. If she could do it again, she would go to ______________.
2. Jack went to ______________. If he could do it again, he would go to ______________.

ONLINE PRACTICE

SPEAK *with* CONFIDENCE

A List three regrets—one from your childhood, one from the last year, and one from the last two weeks.

1. ______________________________
2. ______________________________
3. ______________________________

B **GROUP WORK** Talk with a group about the regrets you listed.

English in Action

ONLINE PRACTICE

1 | Preview

PAIR WORK Look at the photos. How do you think Alex feels in photo a? Why might he feel that way? What are Maria, Alex and Tom doing in photo b? Why do you think they are doing it?

a

b

FEELINGS

17

18

19

20

VIDEO

2 | Practice

A Watch the video. Were your guesses correct?

B Watch the video again. Write A (for Alex), M (for Maria), or B (for both Alex and Maria).

1. ____ is/are stressed out.
2. ____ is/are scared of missing deadlines.
3. ____ can't find a job.
4. ____ would like to be an actor.
5. ____ wish(es) that he/she hadn't studied so much in high school.
6. ____ is/are worried about not having enough money.
7. ____ is/are afraid of public speaking.
8. ____ is/are going to be in a commercial.

3 | Discuss

GROUP WORK Answer the questions.

1. What advice would you give to Alex? To Maria?
2. What causes you the most stress? How do you deal with it?
3. What is your dream job? What would you need to do to get the job? Do you think you'll ever have that job? Why or why not?

CONFIDENCE BOOSTER Student A: Turn to page 86.
Student B: Turn to page 94.

17 Are you afraid of...?

Student A and Student B: Take turns talking about your fears. Your partner suggests ways to overcome each fear. Use the ideas below or your own ideas.

Fear of heights: each day, climb up one more rung of a ladder

Fear of public speaking: practice speaking in front of a pet, then a friend, then a few friends

I can ask about fears.
☐ Very well ☐ I need more practice.

I can talk about fears.
☐ Very well ☐ I need more practice.

See Language Booster page 43.

18 I'm overworked.

Student A and Student B: Take turns discussing these causes of stress. Your partner gives advice by talking about his or her own experiences

financial problems	problems with a family member
too much work	health problems

I can talk about causes of stress.
☐ Very well ☐ I need more practice.

I can give advice by talking about personal experiences.
☐ Very well ☐ I need more practice.

See Language Booster page 45.

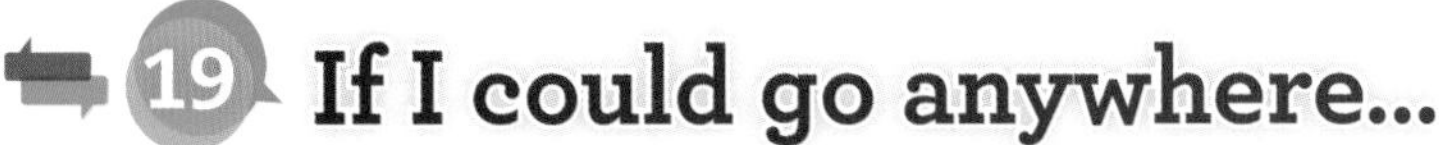

19 If I could go anywhere...

Student A and Student B: Take turns talking about the dreams and wishes below. Your partner expresses interest and asks for reasons.

be a famous actor	stay in a space hotel
create a new social networking site	invent a new type of technology

I can talk about dreams and wishes.
☐ Very well ☐ I need more practice.

I can express interest and ask for reasons.
☐ Very well ☐ I need more practice.

See Language Booster page 47.

20 I wish I had...

Student A and Student B: Look at some of the things that people regret below. Think of two more and write them down. Choose two that you regret the most. Your partner asks about your regrets.

hurting someone's feelings	not making the right decisions

I can ask about regrets.
☐ Very well ☐ I need more practice.

I can talk about regrets.
☐ Very well ☐ I need more practice.

See Language Booster page 49.

21 It started out kind of slow.

- Relating the plot of movies
- Describing reactions to movies

1 | Vocabulary

A Think of movies that you have seen. Write a movie next to each adjective below.

suspenseful		depressing	
slow		heartwarming	
hilarious		corny	
offensive		tearjerker	
moving		nail-biter	

B PAIR WORK Take turns sharing the movies from your chart. Give reasons for your opinions.

2 | Conversation

CD2 12 **A Listen. How does Peter feel about the movie? What is the movie about?**

Jennifer: So, how was the movie you saw last night?

Peter: It started out kind of slow, but by the end, I was really into it.

Jennifer: What was it about?

Peter: It's about this woman whose life completely falls apart. In the beginning, she gets fired from her job. Then she can't pay her rent.

Jennifer: Wow, that sounds really depressing.

Peter: Yeah, but it gets better. She has to live in her car because she doesn't have a place to stay. Meanwhile, someone is looking for her.

Jennifer: Who is this person?

Peter: It's an editor from a publishing company. A few years earlier, she had written a book and sent it to a publisher, but she had never heard anything back.

Jennifer: OK, this is starting to sound more interesting.

Peter: Eventually, the editor finds her and offers her a book deal!

Jennifer: Wow, that's great!

Peter: Yeah, it was a little corny, but it was heartwarming.

B PAIR WORK Practice the conversation

CD2 13 **C Listen. Write the three extra sentences you hear in the conversation. Practice the new conversation.**

3 | Language Booster

A **Notice the ways we relate the plot of movies and describe reactions to movies.**

Relating the plot of movies	Describing reactions to movies
It's about this woman (whose life completely falls apart). In the beginning, (she gets fired from her job). It starts out in (New York City).	It started out kind of slow, but by the end, I was really into it. It was really heartwarming. / gripping. / exciting.

B **PAIR WORK** **Describe the beginning of a movie to your partner.**

Example:

A: I thought the movie was a real nail-biter. It's about this man who is being chased by spies.

B: Wow, that sounds exciting!

A: Yeah, it was. It starts out in New York City.

4 | Pronunciation Pausing when relating stories

CD2 14 **A** **Listen to the movie descriptions. Notice the places where the speaker pauses for a moment.**

A: It starts out in New York City. [pause] The man is walking alone [pause] on a quiet street [pause] when suddenly [pause] he hears a scream!

B: Then what happens?

B **PAIR WORK** **Take turns describing the beginning of a movie, like you did in the Language Booster section, part B above. This time, pay attention to places where you can pause for a moment.**

SPEAK *with* CONFIDENCE

A **PAIR WORK** **Think of a movie that you remember well. Write notes about the main events of the movie.**

Movie title:
It's about
In the beginning,
Later on,
Eventually,
Finally,

Disney · PIXAR
UP
MAY 29
DISNEY DIGITAL
3D

B **GROUP WORK** **Take turns describing your movie.**

22 It has a really good beat.

- Describing music
- Joining discussions

1 | Vocabulary

A Think of songs that you have heard. Write a song next to the descriptive words below.

____________ beat	____________ poetic lyrics
____________ catchy tune	____________ romantic
____________ danceable	____________ mellow
____________ upbeat	____________ melancholy

B PAIR WORK Share your answers with a partner. Give two reasons for your answers.

2 | Conversation

CD2 15 **A Listen to a conversation about music. What kind of song does Mike like? Why doesn't Carlo really like the song?**

Mike: Hey, I just downloaded this new song. Listen. It's really mellow. Isn't it great?

Carlo: It's a nice song, but I actually prefer more upbeat music.

Mike: Have you paid attention to the lyrics, though? They're really poetic.

Trina: Oh, are you guys talking about Adele's new song?

Mike: Yeah, do you like it?

Trina: It's great! She has the most amazing voice.

Carlo: I want you guys to listen to a song that I just downloaded. It's really danceable.

Mike: This song is great. It has a really good beat.

Trina: Yeah, I think I'll download it, too.

B PAIR WORK Practice the conversation.

CD2 16 **C Listen. Write the three extra sentences you hear in the conversation. Practice the new conversation.**

pair with VOCABULARY WORKSHEET 22

3 | Language Booster

A Notice the ways we describe music and join discussions.

Describing music	Joining discussions
It has a good beat. / It has a catchy tune. The lyrics are provocative. It's really mellow. It's a little melancholy.	Oh, are you guys talking about (Adele's) new song? Hey, did I hear you mention something about (Adele)? (She) just released a new album, didn't (she)?

B **PAIR WORK** Describe a new song that you just heard to a partner.

Example:

A: Have you heard the song…? It's really romantic.

B: Yeah, I have. I like it, but it's a little melancholy. Do you like the song…?

POP CULTURE 22

4 | Pronunciation Syllable stress in longer words

CD2 17 **A** Listen to the pronunciation of these longer words. Notice the syllable stress.

1. **mel**ancholy 2. ro**man**tic 3. po**e**tic 4. **dance**able 5. pro**voc**ative

B **PAIR WORK** Describe a song to a partner like you did in the Language Booster section, part B above. This time, pay attention to the syllable stress in long words.

ONLINE PRACTICE

SPEAK *with* CONFIDENCE

A List three songs that you like and write words that describe them.

Names of songs	Words that describe the songs
1.	
2.	
3.	

B **GROUP WORK** Work in a group of three and discuss the songs you described in above. Take turns joining the discussion.

23 Did you hear about...?

- Asking about trends
- Describing trends

1 | Vocabulary

A Complete each sentence below with the name of a celebrity or someone you know personally.

1. ____________ **follows the fads** / **is trendy.**
2. ____________ shops a lot for clothes that are **in** / **in style** / **stylish** / **up to date.**
3. ____________ likes to wear **vintage** / **retro** clothing.
4. ____________ always looks **fashionable** / **chic.**
5. ____________ likes to wear **modern** clothes.
6. ____________ is a **trendsetter.**
7. ____________ never wears clothes that are **out** / **out of style** / **outdated.**

B PAIR WORK Take turns sharing and giving reasons for your ideas.

2 | Conversation

CD2 18 **A** Listen. What does Jodie say is in style? What does she say is out of style?

Lynn: Thanks for going shopping with me, Jodie. I really need new clothes, and you always look so fashionable.
Jodie: Oh, thanks, Lynn. It's really no problem. _____
Lynn: Well, you are a trendsetter.

Lynn: What do you think of these pants? _____
Jodie: Well, these days, a lot of people are wearing really bright pants.
Lynn: Really? _____
Jodie: Yeah, but you shouldn't follow a fad that you're not comfortable with.

Lynn: How about skirts?
Jodie: The current trend is to wear shorter skirts.
Lynn: Are knee-length skirts out of style?
Jodie: Yeah. Knee-length skirts are outdated.
Lynn: Wow, I really do need help. _____

B PAIR WORK Practice the conversation. Then find the best places to add the sentences below to the conversation and practice it again.

1. I have so many knee-length skirts.
2. I wouldn't feel comfortable in bright pants.
3. I love to shop for clothes!
4. Do you think they would look good on me?

pair with VOCABULARY WORKSHEET 23

3 | Language Booster

A Notice the ways we ask about and describe trends.

Asking about trends	Describing trends
What's currently in style?	These days, a lot of people are wearing (really bright pants).
What's considered trendy right now?	Nowadays, it's trendy to wear / The current trend is to wear — shorter skirts.
Is it out of style to wear (knee-length skirts)?	

B **PAIR WORK** Look at the trends below. Tell your partner if you think the trend is in style.

baggy pants   oversized shirts   big jewelry   metallic-colored shoes

4 | Listening

CD2 19 **A** Listen. Allie is cleaning out her closet. Write down the types of clothing mentioned in the conversation.

Clothing	Allie wants to keep it	Allie wants to get rid of it

CD2 19 **B** Listen again. Check the correct column for each type of clothing.

SPEAK *with* CONFIDENCE

A Brainstorm a list of clothing types that are currently in style for men, women, or both men and women.

pants: *skinny jeans, wide-leg jeans*
shoes:
jackets:
hats:
other:

B **GROUP WORK** Ask and answer questions about the clothing types that you've listed above. Discuss what is in style and what is out of style.

POP CULTURE 23

24 Have you heard...?

- Sharing surprising news
- Expressing surprise

1 | Vocabulary

A Read the article in a celebrity gossip magazine. Complete the sentences with the words in the box.

apparently	(be) with	break up (with)	(juicy) gossip
paparazzi	scandal	spotted	the latest

Is this the end of Brantonia?

Have you heard ________(1) about everyone's favorite celebrity couple? It looks like this might be the end of the pair we know as Brantonia. According to my sources, Antonia wants to ________(2) Brad! She was ________(3) last night with another famous actor you might know. What a ________(4)!

There's also a big rumor going around about Brad. ________(5), he isn't as innocent as he seems. Some ________(6) snapped photos of him last night accompanied by Santana Grace. Is he ________(7) Santana now? Should we start calling them Brantana? Thanks for reading my blog. Come back tomorrow for more ________(8)!

B PAIR WORK Discuss celebrity gossip magazines, websites, and blogs. Do you like them? Why do you think people like to read them?

2 | Conversation

CD2 20 **A Listen. Who is the gossip about? What happened?**

Brian: Have you heard the latest on the band The Dream Captains? It's a huge scandal.

Matt: No, what happened? ____

Brian: Well, apparently, the lead singer was arrested last night. He was spotted trying to rob a store! ____

Matt: No way! Is that for real? ____

Brian: I read about it on a couple of different gossip sites. But of course, it might just be a rumor. ____

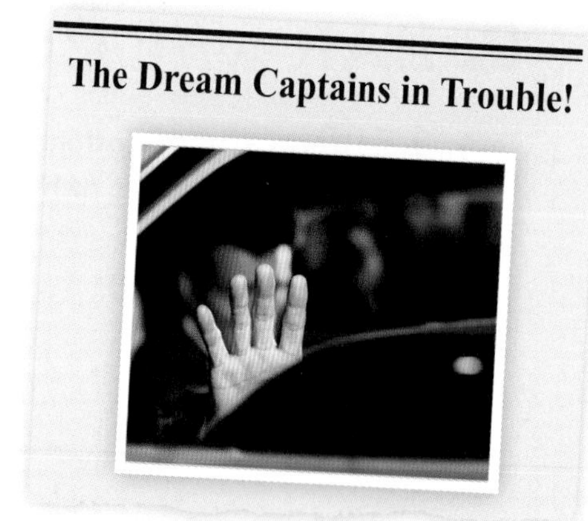
The Dream Captains in Trouble!

B PAIR WORK Practice the conversation. Then find the best places to add the sentences below to the conversation and practice it again.

1. He has so much money.
3. I really like their music.
2. We'll have to wait to find out.
4. He tried to walk out of the store with clothes!

3 | Language Booster

A **Notice the ways we share surprising news and express surprise.**

Sharing surprising news	Expressing surprise
Have you heard the latest on (the band The Dream Captains)?	No way! Is that for real?
Did you know that…?	You've got to be kidding!
Guess what!	You can't be serious!
Wait till you hear this …	That's amazing.

B **PAIR WORK** **Share one surprising piece of news with your partner.**

Example:

A: Did you know that a man found a bear inside his home yesterday?

B: No way! How did that happen?

4 | Listening

CD2 21 **A** **Listen to people share surprising news. Then number the headlines from 1 to 4 in the order that you hear the stories.**

_____ a. Missing Actor Reappears

_____ b. Child Actor Loses Fortune

_____ c. Former Athlete Turns to Fashion

_____ d. Cheating Athlete Gets Caught!

CD2 21 **B** **Listen again. Take notes on two of the stories. Then choose one of the stories and summarize it for your partner. Make sure you each summarize a different story.**

ONLINE PRACTICE

SPEAK *with* CONFIDENCE

A **Think of a surprising story that you heard recently. Write the main points of the story below.**

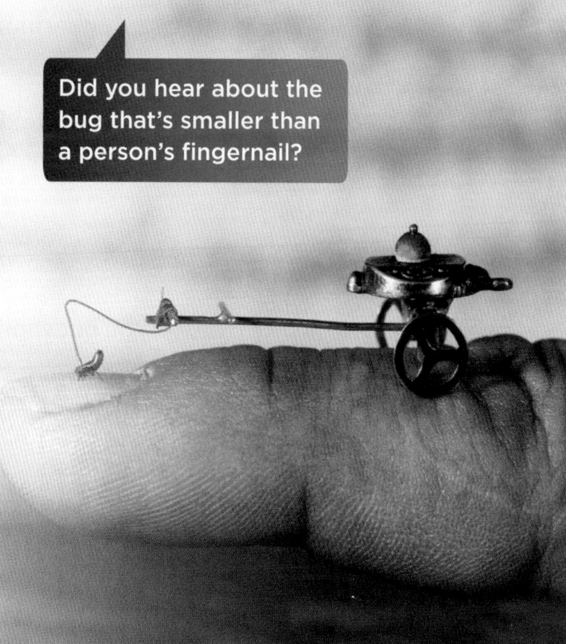

Did you hear about the bug that's smaller than a person's fingernail?

B **PAIR WORK** **Share your surprising news with a partner.**

English in Action

ONLINE PRACTICE

POP CULTURE

21

22

23

24

VIDEO

1 | Preview

PAIR WORK Look at the photos and answer the questions.

1. What do Maria and Tom think of Alex's clothes?
2. What do you think of Alex's clothes?
3. What do Maria and Alex think of Tom's clothes?
4. What do you think of Tom's clothes?

2 | Practice

A Watch the video. Mark the statements T (true) or F (false).

_____ 1. Alex and Kate are going to take some clients out to dinner. _____

_____ 2. Alex is nervous about the dinner with the clients. _____

_____ 3. Maria knows a lot about popular culture. _____

_____ 4. Alex often watches new movies. _____

_____ 5. Maria helped Tom shop for some new clothes. _____

_____ 6. Kate is interested in fashion. _____

B Watch the video again. Rewrite the false sentences, so they are true.

3 | Discuss

GROUP WORK Answer the questions.

1. Maria suggests that Alex talk with his clients about music and movies. What else do you think he should talk about?
2. Do you follow the trends? Why or why not?
3. Do you think it's important to follow popular culture? Why or why not?

CONFIDENCE BOOSTER Student A: Turn to page 87.
Student B: Turn to page 95.

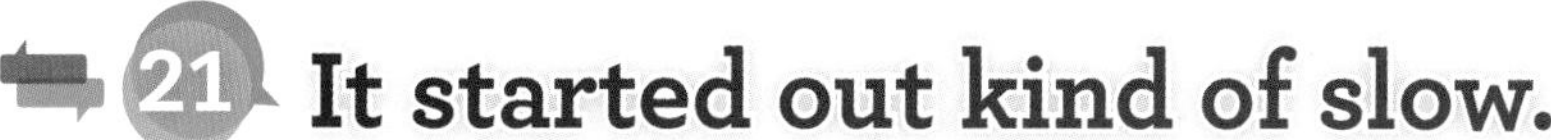

21 It started out kind of slow.

Student A and Student B: Take turns describing movies that you've seen. Describe movies that fit the descriptions below.

a heartwarming drama	a corny romantic comedy
a hilarious comedy	a suspenseful nail-biter

I can relate the plot of movies.
☐ Very well ☐ I need more practice.

I can describe reactions to movies.
☐ Very well ☐ I need more practice.

See Language Booster page 53.

22 It has a really good beat.

Student A and Student B: Discuss a songs that you know that fit the descriptions below.
Student C: Join the conversation.

is poetic and melancholy	is upbeat and has a catchy tune
has a good beat and is danceable	is romantic and mellow

I can describe music.
☐ Very well ☐ I need more practice.

I can join discussions.
☐ Very well ☐ I need more practice.

See Language Booster page 55.

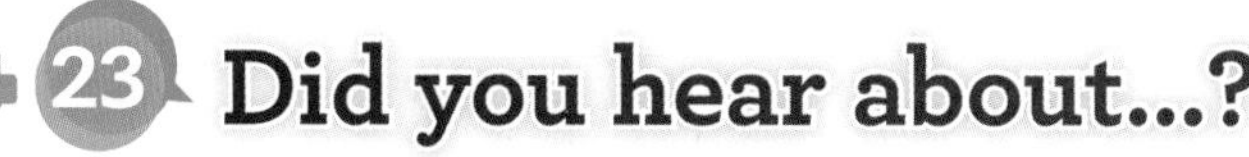

23 Did you hear about...?

Student A and Student B: Imagine it is twenty years from now. Ask about and describe the current and future trends for the things below.

a type of pants	a type of shoes	trendy colors	a type of coat

I can ask about trends.
☐ Very well ☐ I need more practice.

I can describe trends.
☐ Very well ☐ I need more practice.

See Language Booster page 57.

24 Have you heard...?

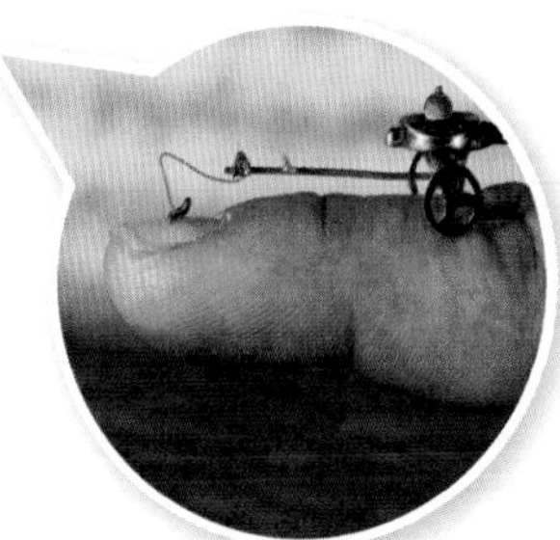

A Student A and Student B: Take turns sharing the news headlines below and expressing surprise.

Sugar is Actually Good for Your Health!
No Rainfall for an Entire Year!

B Now change roles. Student B gives a presentation and Student A asks follow-up questions.

I can share surprising news.
☐ Very well ☐ I need more practice.

I can express surprise.
☐ Very well ☐ I need more practice.

See Language Booster page 59.

25 Is the flight on time?

- Checking in at the airport
- Confirming information

1 | Vocabulary

A Circle the correct word to complete each sentence.

1. I always try to get a **window seat / an aisle seat** because I like to look at the clouds during the flight.
2. I have a coach ticket. How much do I have to pay to **upgrade / board** to business class?
3. When you sit at a **gate / a terminal / an emergency exit row**, you have to be strong enough to help people off the plane if there is an accident.
4. If you don't want to carry heavy bags on the plane with you, you can **use your boarding pass / check your luggage / take a carry-on bag**.
5. You can put small bags and coats in the **security check / overhead bin**.

B PAIR WORK Take turns talking about your travel preferences.

2 | Conversation

CD2 22 **A Listen. Does Nicolas want an aisle seat or a window seat? How much luggage does Nicolas have?**

Airline employee: May I have your passport, please?

Nicolas: Yes, here it is.

Airline employee: Thank you. Let's see. Would you like a window seat or an aisle seat?

Nicolas: I'd prefer a window seat, please.

Airline employee: OK. I have a window seat in row 12. Are you checking any luggage?

Nicolas: Yes, I'd like to check two pieces of luggage.

Airline employee: OK. Here is your boarding pass.

Nicolas: Thank you. My flight is leaving from Gate 14, right?

Airline employee: Yes, your flight is departing from Gate 14. Enjoy your flight!

B PAIR WORK Practice the conversation.

CD2 23 **C Listen. Write the three extra sentences you hear in the conversation. Practice the new conversation.**

pair with VOCABULARY WORKSHEET 25

3 | Language Booster

A Notice the things an airline employee might say when we check in at the airport and ways we can confirm information.

Checking in at the airport	Confirming information
Are you checking any luggage?	My flight is leaving from (Gate 14), right?
Your flight is departing from (Gate 14).	Dinner will be served on this flight, won't it?
You'll be seated in an emergency exit row.	Is the flight on time?
Walk down the hall and go through security.	

B PAIR WORK Role-play a conversation between an airline employee and a customer. Ask about checking luggage and gate numbers.

Examples:

A: Are you checking any luggage

B: Yes, I'm checking … My flight is leaving from Gate…?

4 | Pronunciation Stress in two-syllable words

CD2 24 **A** Listen to people asking questions at an airport. Notice the stress is on the first syllable of many two-syllable words.

1. Is this an international **air**port?
2. Are you **check**ing any **lug**gage?
3. Do you mind **sit**ting in an emergency **ex**it row?
4. Would you like a **win**dow seat?
5. Do I have to go through **cus**toms?

B PAIR WORK Ask and answer the questions above. Pay attention to syllable stress in two-syllable words.

SPEAK *with* CONFIDENCE

A Write answers to the questions below.

You are a customer:	You are an airline employee:
1. Are you checking luggage?	1. What gate does the customer's flight leave from?
2. Where do you prefer to sit?	2. Is the flight delayed or on time?
	3. Will dinner be served on the flight?

B PAIR WORK Role-play a conversation between an airline employee and a customer. Take turns checking in to an airport. Use the information above.

26 I'm afraid...

- Reporting bad news
- Asking for help or advice

1 | Vocabulary

A Complete the blog post below with the words in the box.

a. canceled	c. down	e. misplaced	g. stolen
b. damaged	d. expired	f. missed	h. vacancy

Travels with Tina

My travel has been tough! First, I ___1___ my flight to Auckland, New Zealand. The computers at the airport were ___2___, so I tried to make a new reservation on my phone, but I dropped my phone on the floor and it was ___3___. I arrived in Sydney, the airline ___4___ my luggage. And all the hotels were full! After four hours, I finally found a hotel with a ___5___. When I went to register at the hotel, I discovered that my wallet was ___6___. I did have an extra credit card in my backpack. I looked at it and it was ___7___! I called my bank to report my wallet stolen and ___8___ all my credit cards. I unpacked my backpack, and guess what I found—my wallet!

B PAIR WORK Take turns telling each other about a bad traveling experience.

2 | Conversation

CD2 25 **A Listen. Where does Victoria want to go? What three problems did Victoria have?**

Victoria: Hi, I have to transfer to Flight 734 to São Paulo.

Airline employee: I'm sorry to inform you that the flight has been canceled.

Victoria: Oh, no! Can you rebook me on the next flight?

Airline employee: You just missed the last flight of the day. The next flight is in two days.

Hotel employee: I hate to tell you this, but we don't have any vacancies.

Victoria: Well, could you please recommend another hotel nearby?

Hotel employee: Sure, there are several hotels on Hotel Drive. The best thing to do is to go online.

Victoria: Thank you.

Victoria: Excuse me. Do I need a password to get online here at the airport?

Airport employee: No, but I'm afraid our network is down at the moment.

Victoria: This is not my day! Do you know of any Internet cafes nearby?

Airport employee: No, I'm sorry. I don't. But you can use my phone to find a hotel.

B PAIR WORK Practice the conversation.

CD2 26 **C Listen. Write the three extra sentences you hear in the conversation. Practice the new conversation.**

3 | Language Booster

A **Notice the ways we report bad news and ask for help or advice.**

Reporting bad news		Asking for help or advice	
I hate to tell you this, but I'm sorry to inform you that Unfortunately, I'm afraid	the flight has been canceled.	Could you please Can you	recommend another hotel?
		Would it be possible to (use your phone)? Do you know of (any internet cafes nearby)?	

B **PAIR WORK** **Report a piece of bad news to your partner. Your partner will ask for help or advice.**

Example:

A: Unfortunately, your passport has expired.

B: Oh, no! Would it be possible to…?

4 | Listening

CD2 27 **A** **Listen to people give bad news and ask for help or advice. Then number the people's problems in the order that you hear the conversations.**

_____ a. The speaker missed her flight.

_____ b. The speaker's credit card was stolen.

_____ c. The hotel doesn't have any vacancies.

_____ d. The speaker's luggage was damaged.

CD2 27 **B** **Listen again. Write down on a piece of paper how each person's problem was solved.**

C **GROUP WORK** **Discuss how each person's problem was solved. Do you think they were good solutions?**

ONLINE PRACTICE

SPEAK *with* CONFIDENCE

A **Write down four possible problems that people might have while they are travelling.**

1. ______________________________
2. ______________________________
3. ______________________________
4. ______________________________

B **PAIR WORK** **Share your problems above with your partner. Then take turns reporting bad news and asking for help or advice.**

27 Do you think...?

- Comparing and contrasting alternatives
- Giving reasons for choices

1 | Vocabulary

A Check the travel options that you prefer.

Do you prefer...?
☐ to see the big **tourist attractions**, ☐ to **go off the beaten path**, or ☐ to **lounge around**?
☐ to take a **guided tour** or ☐ to **explore** on your own?
☐ to plan and **book things in advance** or ☐ to **keep your options open**?
☐ to **splurge** or ☐ to **stick to a budget**?
☐ a **bed and breakfast**, ☐ a **hostel**, ☐ a **luxury hotel**, or ☐ a **budget hotel**?

B **PAIR WORK** Take turns sharing your travel preferences.

2 | Conversation

CD2 28 **A** Listen. Where are May and Alicia? What options do they discuss and prefer?

Alicia: I'm so glad we came to London. It's such a beautiful city.

May: It really is. I can't wait to explore!

Alicia: What do you feel like doing? Do you want to take a guided tour or explore on our own?

May: Oh, I'd rather explore on our own. Guided tours are too crowded.

Alicia: I agree. Hm...what should we have for breakfast?

May: Do you think we should splurge or stick to our budget?

Alicia: I think it makes sense to splurge. I mean, you only live once!

May: Well, that's true.

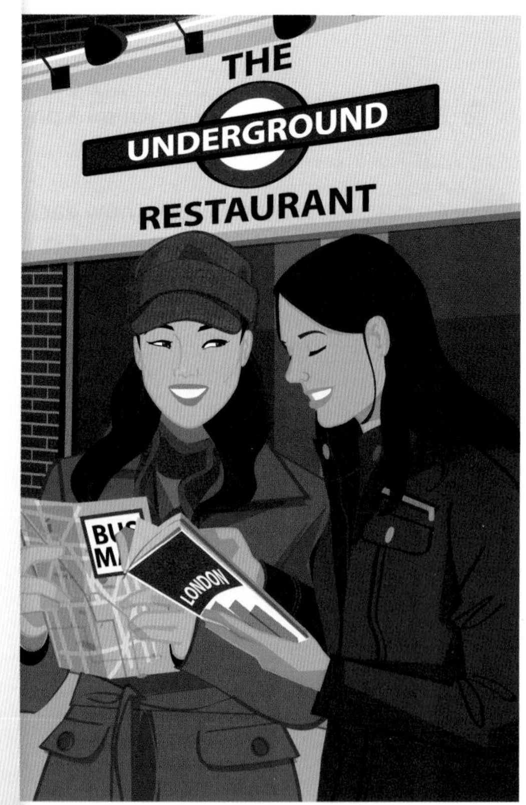

B **PAIR WORK** Practice the conversation.

CD2 29 **C** Listen. Write the three extra sentences you hear in the conversation. Practice the new conversation.

pair with VOCABULARY WORKSHEET 27

3 | Language Booster

A Notice the ways we compare and contrast alternatives and give reasons for our choices.

Comparing and contrasting alternatives	Giving reasons for choices
What do you feel like doing? Do you want to take a guided tour or explore on our own?	I'd rather explore on our own. Guided tours are too crowded.
Do you think we should splurge or stick to our budget?	I think it makes sense to splurge. I mean, you only live once!
Which do you want to do, make reservations in advance or keep our options open?	It would probably be a good idea to make reservations in advance. We'll be travelling during the busy tourist season, and the hotels might fill up.

B PAIR WORK Imagine you are on vacation. Ask your partner what he or she feels like doing today. Offer two choices.

Example:

A: What do you feel like doing? Do you want to see a movie or hang out at the mall?

B: I'd rather hang out at the mall. I need to buy a new pair of sneakers.

TRAVEL 27

4 | Pronunciation Linking with -s

CD2 30 **A Listen to the sentences. Notice the link between the words that end with *-s* and the words that follow them.**

1. I think we should keep our option**s o**pen.
2. Guided tour**s a**re too crowded.
3. The hotel**s m**ight fill up.
4. Let'**s m**ake reservation**s i**n advance.

B PAIR WORK Ask a new partner what he or she feels like doing today, like you did in Language Booster section, part B. This time, pay attention to linking words that end in *-s*.

ONLINE PRACTICE

SPEAK *with* CONFIDENCE

A Write three alternatives for things that people might do on vacation.

1. ____________ 2. ____________ 3. ____________

Which do you want to do, on a guided tour or explore on our own?

I'd rather go on a guided tour. That way we won't waste any time!

B PAIR WORK Compare and contrast the alternatives that you wrote above with your partner. Give reasons for your choices.

28 It's important to...

- Describing cultural differences
- Explaining why something is a problem

1 | Vocabulary

A Write answers to the questions below on a separate piece of paper.

1. Is it **acceptable** to arrive late to a meeting in your culture?
2. What is an **inappropriate** thing to do at a meeting?
3. What is one **insensitive** thing that you shouldn't talk about with people you've just met?
4. Is it **inconsiderate** to arrive at a dinner party ten minutes late?
5. Is it **customary** to give gifts at a business meeting?
6. What is the worst cultural **faux pas** you've ever made?
7. What is the most important thing a visitor should **be aware of** when visiting your home country?

B PAIR WORK Discuss your answers to the questions above with a partner. Give reasons for your answers.

2 | Conversation

CD2 31 **A Listen. Where is Patrick going to go? What cultural advice does Sophie give Patrick?**

Sophie Are you excited about your trip to New York?

Patrick: Yeah, I really am, but I'm a little nervous, too. It's my first time in the United States, and I want to make sure I don't make any faux pas.

Sophie: Oh, I see. What are you not sure about? _____

Patrick: Well, I have an early morning business meeting the day after I arrive. Is it acceptable to arrive a little late? _____

Sophie: Not really. In the U.S., it's important to be on time. _____

Patrick: OK, that's good to know. What should I do when I first meet people? Should I shake hands? Kiss them?

Sophie: Well, in the U.S., it's inappropriate to kiss people when you first meet them. It's customary to shake hands when you meet people. _____

Patrick: I'm glad I asked.

B PAIR WORK Practice the conversation. Then find the best places to add the sentences below to the conversation and practice it again.

1. You usually also do that at the end of a meeting.
2. Maybe I can help.
3. I'm going to be really tired after my long flight.
4. Being late is seen as inconsiderate.

3 | Language Booster

A **Notice the ways we describe cultural differences and explain why something is a problem.**

Describing cultural differences	Explaining why something is a problem
In the U.S., it's important to be on time.	Being late is seen as inconsiderate.
It's inappropriate to kiss people when you first meet them.	It's customary to shake hands.
It's insensitive to ask someone how much money they make.	That's considered to be personal information.

B **PAIR WORK** **Think of a culture you know about. Describe something that people shouldn't do when visiting that culture and explain why it is a problem.**

Example:

A: In Japan, you shouldn't wear shoes into someone's house. People in Japan usually take their shoes off at the door.

B: In South Korea, it's also customary to take off your shoes at the door.

TRAVEL 28

4 | Listening

CD2 32 **A** **Listen to people talk about cultural faux pas. Then number the pictures in the order that you hear the situations.**

CD2 32 **B** **Listen again. Write down on a piece of paper what you think each person should have done.**

C **GROUP WORK** **Discuss what each person should have done in the situations.**

SPEAK *with* CONFIDENCE

A **Think of your culture. Write three things that you should not do in your culture.**

1. ______________________________
2. ______________________________
3. ______________________________

B **GROUP WORK** **Describe the faux pas you wrote above and the reasons why they are a problem.**

C **CLASS ACTIVITY** **Present one faux pas from the group to the class.**

English in Action

ONLINE PRACTICE

1 | Preview

PAIR WORK **Alex is reading an article about how to woo (impress) clients. What advice do you think the article gives? Check (✓) your guesses.**

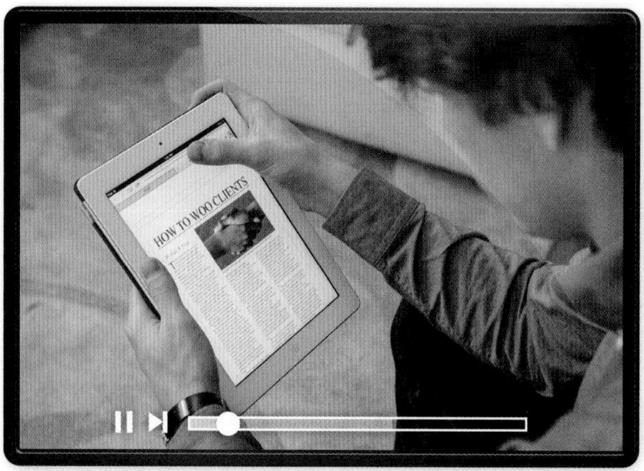

_____ Take them out to a nice restaurant.

_____ Have a firm handshake.

_____ Buy them gifts.

_____ Speak loudly.

_____ Copy their gestures.

_____ Ask about their families.

2 | Practice

A **Watch the video. Were your guesses correct? What other advice did the article give?**

B **Watch the video again. How does Alex try to impress the clients? Check (✓) your answers.**

_____ 1. He takes them out to dinner at a nice restaurant.

_____ 2. He has a firm handshake.

_____ 3. He gives them some gifts.

_____ 4. He tidies up and redecorates his work space.

_____ 5. He introduces them to the president of his company.

_____ 6. He picks them up at the airport.

_____ 7. He copies their gestures.

_____ 8. He changes his clothes.

3 | Discuss

GROUP WORK **Answer the questions.**

1. Do you think Alex impressed the clients? Why or why not?
2. What do you think are good ways to woo clients? What are some other ways to impress clients?
3. Have you ever had to entertain visitors that you didn't know very well? Where did you go? What did you do?

CONFIDENCE BOOSTER Student A: Turn to page 88.
Student B: Turn to page 96.

25 Is the flight on time?

Student A and Student B: Take turns role-playing an airline employee and a customer. Use the information below.

Student A's flight:	Student B's flight:
Flight to New York	Flight to Barcelona
Leaves from Gate 93	Leaves from Gate B2
The flight is on time.	The flight is delayed six hours.
Dinner is not served on the flight.	There are no window or aisle seats left.

I can check in at an airport.
☐ Very well ☐ I need more practice.

I can confirm information.
☐ Very well ☐ I need more practice.

See Language Booster page 63.

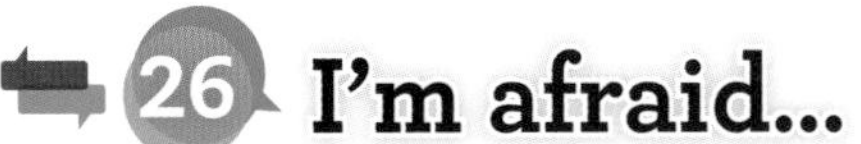

26 I'm afraid...

Student A and Student B: Take turns reporting bad news and asking for help or advice. Use the problems below or think of your own.

Your luggage was stolen. The hotel misplaced your passport.

I can report bad news.
☐ Very well ☐ I need more practice.

I can ask for help or advice.
☐ Very well ☐ I need more practice.

See Language Booster page 65.

27 Do you think...?

Student A and Student B: Take turns asking about the alternatives below and giving reasons for your choices.

go to a spa or go for a hike go to a museum or go shopping

I can compare and contrast alternatives.
☐ Very well ☐ I need more practice.

I can give reasons for my choices.
☐ Very well ☐ I need more practice.

See Language Booster page 67.

28 It's important to...

Student A and Student B: Take turns describing the cultural faux pas below and explaining why they are a problem.

talking about politics or religion
arriving at a dinner party with an expensive gift

I can describe cultural differences.
☐ Very well ☐ I need more practice.

I can explain why something is a problem.
☐ Very well ☐ I need more practice.

See Language Booster page 69.

ONLINE PRACTICE

29 Did you see the game?

- Talking about sporting events
- Changing the subject

1 | Vocabulary

A Complete the article with the correct words in the box.

close
ejected
blowout
overtime
quarter
referee
shot
half-time
outscored
tied

The Day in Sports by Kara Lee

Last night's basketball game between the Boston Celtics and Los Angeles Lakers was a thriller! With ten seconds left in the game, the score was ______________. The Lakers attempted a ______________ at the basket but missed it. The game then went into ______________, and the Celtics ______________ the Lakers and won the ballgame.

The game between the New York Knicks and Miami Heat last night wasn't nearly as ______________ as the Celtics-Lakers game. During the first ______________, Miami's best player was ______________ from the game for arguing with the ______________. At ______________, the score was close, but the Knicks ended up getting a ______________ win, with a final score of 121–98.

In World Cup news, Brazil defeated Germany with just one goal scored in

B PAIR WORK Would you rather watch your favorite team win in a blowout or a close game? Why?

2 | Conversation

CD2 33 **A Listen. What kind of game is Robert talking about? What is Tristan talking about?**

Robert: Did you see the match?

Tristan: The match? What match?

Robert: Uh...the World Cup? The biggest soccer tournament in the world? Brazil was incredible!

Tristan: Oh? That's great. So, do you know what kind of car that is?

Robert: Uh, not sure. So yeah, it was a really close match. At the end of the second half, the score was tied, so the match went into overtime. Then Brazil had this penalty kick, and...

Tristan: Did they? Speaking of overtime, did I mention how much I've been working lately?

B PAIR WORK Practice the conversation.

CD2 34 **C Listen. Write the three extra sentences you hear in the conversation. Practice the new conversation.**

pair with VOCABULARY WORKSHEET 29

3 | Language Booster

A Notice the ways we talk about sporting events and change the subject.

Talking about sporting events	Changing the subject
Did you see the game?	So yeah, (it was a really close match).
Who were you rooting for?	Speaking of (overtime, I've been working so much).
It was a blowout.	So anyway, / That reminds me, — I've had a lot of work.
It went into overtime.	
It was incredible!	

B PAIR WORK Take turns starting a conversation about a sporting event and changing the subject.

Example:

A: Did you see the game last night? It was incredible!

B: Oh, speaking of games, do you want to come over and play my new video game?

4 | Pronunciation Intonation to convey extreme emotion

CD2 35 **A Listen to the sentences. Notice that the positive emotional statements end in a raised intonation, and negative emotional statements end in lowered intonation.**

1. You should have seen it!
2. It was incredible!
3. Their best player was ejected!
4. My favorite team lost!

B PAIR WORK Take turns saying negative and positive emotional statements to your partner. Pay attention to your sentence intonation.

ONLINE PRACTICE

SPEAK *with* CONFIDENCE

A Have you been to any sports events? Write down any sports events you've been to or have seen on TV. Write down why it was memorable.

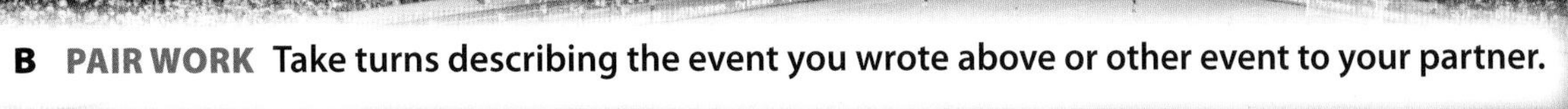

B PAIR WORK Take turns describing the event you wrote above or other event to your partner.

30 Hold on.

- Interrupting to ask for clarification
- Clarifying

1 | Vocabulary

A Read the news story below.

Last night, police officers **arrested** a **criminal** who they believe is responsible for a series of burglaries they have been **investigating** for months. The man is known to **break into** homes and **force** his way in. **Victims** reported that they were missing jewelry. A **witness** saw something **suspicious** in her neighbor's house and called the police. It turns out that the criminal was a 90-year-old man!

B PAIR WORK Take turns summarizing the news story above to your partner.

2 | Conversation

CD2 36 **A** Listen. What did the man try to steal? What happened to the man?

Nina: Did you read about this guy who tried to steal a car yesterday? _____

Erika: What do you mean he "tried" to steal it?

Nina: He forced a woman out of the car in front of witnesses, but he didn't know how to drive it! So, he asked the woman to show him how to drive the car.

Erika: Hold on. What did you say the guy did?

Nina: He actually asked the woman to come back to the car to show him how to start it. _____

Erika: No way! What did the woman do? _____

Nina: She ran away and called the police! When the police arrived, the guy was still trying to figure out how to start the car! _____

B PAIR WORK Practice the conversation. Then find the best places to add the sentences below to the conversation and practice it again.

1. They arrested him and took him to jail!	3. Did she show him how to start the car?
2. It's an unbelievable story.	4. Isn't that ridiculous?

3 | Language Booster

A **Notice the ways we interrupt to ask for clarification and to clarify.**

Interrupting to ask for clarification	Clarifying
What do you mean / Wait, did you say that — he "tried" to steal it?	Well, what happened was (he knew how to drive, but he didn't know how to drive a hybrid).
Hold on. What did you say (the guy) did?	(He) actually (asked the woman to come back to the car to show him how to start it).

B **PAIR WORK** **Take turns telling each other about something that happened to you last week. Your partner will ask for clarification, and you will clarify.**

4 | Listening

CD2 37 **A** **Listen to a conversation about something that happened in the news. Mark the statements T (true) or F (false).**

_____ 1. A woman stole a laptop from her neighbor.

_____ 2. The woman tried to sell the laptop to her friend.

_____ 3. The woman told the truth to the neighbor.

_____ 4. The woman's neighbor took the laptop away from her and walked away with it.

_____ 5. The woman called the police to arrest the man who took the laptop from her.

CD2 38 **B** **Listen to the rest of the conversation and write answers to the questions.**

1. How did the owner of the laptop prove that it was his? ____________________

2. What happened to the woman? ____________________

ONLINE PRACTICE

SPEAK *with* CONFIDENCE

A **Write notes about a strange crime that you heard about, or make up your own crime story.**

B **PAIR WORK** **Tell your partner your crime story. Your partner will ask for clarification. After you tell your story, your partner will guess whether your story was real or made up.**

31 Studies have shown...

- Giving evidence to support opinions
- Giving examples to support opinions

1 | Vocabulary

A Write down answers to the questions below on a separate piece of paper.

1. Do you think **banner ads** and **pop-up ads** can persuade **consumers** to buy certain products?
2. Do you ever find yourself humming or singing **jingles** from TV **advertisements**? If yes, which ones?
3. Do you remember any **slogans** from advertisements? If yes, which ones?
4. How do you decide which **brands** to buy? List three things that affect your choices.
5. Do you think advertisements **influence** your **buying habits**? Why or why not?
6. What kinds of things do you think advertisers do to try to **manipulate** consumers?

B PAIR WORK Share your answers to the questions above. Give reasons for your answers.

2 | Conversation

CD2 39 **A Listen. What does Luiz think of banner ads at the beginning of the conversation? What does he think of them at the end of the conversation?**

Luiz: These banner ads are so annoying. I don't know why advertising companies create them. _____

Kim: Actually, I read somewhere that banner ads do influence consumers.

Luiz: Really? But I don't even pay attention to them. I only see them for half a second. _____

Kim: I know. Me, too. But it's been proven that if you see the same thing many times, it can affect you even if you don't pay attention to it.

Luiz: Is that really true? _____

Kim: Well, studies have shown that if you keep seeing a banner ad over and over, you develop a positive feeling about that brand or product. For example, people tend to remember banner ads and they tend to shop for those brands.

Luiz: Wow, I didn't realize that advertisements could manipulate consumers that much. _____

B PAIR WORK Practice the conversation. Then find the best places to add the sentences below to the conversation and practice it again.

1. I'll have to pay more attention to them!	3. I'm sure they don't have any effect on consumers.
2. Then I scroll down and they disappear from my screen.	4. It's hard to believe.

3 | Language Booster

A Notice the ways we give evidence and examples to support opinions.

Giving evidence to support opinions	
Studies have shown I've heard that I read somewhere that It's been proven that	people tend to remember banner ads and they tend to shop for those brands.

Giving examples to support opinions	
For instance, Like you know how It's like when For example,	if you keep seeing a banner ad over and over, you develop a positive feeling about that brand or product on the right side.

B GROUP WORK Look at the statements below. Agree or disagree with the statements. Give evidence and examples to support your opinions.

Advertisements are honest. There is too much advertising nowadays.

4 | Listening

CD2 40 **A** Listen to people give their opinions about ads. For each speaker, check *Supports opinion well* or *Doesn't support opinion well.*

	Supports opinion well	Doesn't support opinion well
1.		
2.		
3.		

CD2 40 **B** Listen again. Think about the speakers for who you checked *Doesn't support opinion well.* What kind of evidence or examples do you think might help each speaker support his or her opinion better? Discuss your answers with a partner.

SPEAK *with* CONFIDENCE

ONLINE PRACTICE

A In your opinion, what is more effective—funny advertisements or sad advertisements? Why?

Your opinion:
Evidence and examples:

B GROUP WORK Work in a group of six—in each group, two to three people should think funny ads are more influential, and two to three should think sad ads are more influential. Express and support your opinions.

32 What's your opinion?

- Asking for opinions about issues
- Politely giving opinions

1 | Vocabulary

A Check the issues that you think your city should spend money on. Add two of your own ideas.

My city should...

____ 1. **reduce** crime.

____ 2. **increase** the number of schools

____ 3. **repair potholes** in the streets

____ 4. **improve** the downtown area

____ 5. **repair** city buildings

____ 6. **increase** the **budget** for parks

____ 7. control **overcrowding**

____ 8. provide **cost-effective** housing

B PAIR WORK Share your answers from part A above. Give reasons for your answers.

2 | Conversation

CD2 41 **A** Listen. What does Citizen 1 want the city to spend money on? What does Citizen 2 want the city to spend money on?

News announcer: We're here in front of City Hall today where citizens are waiting to join a town meeting about next year's budget. Everyone here has an opinion about what the city should be spending money on. Some want more money for schools. Others want better roads.

News announcer: Good evening. City officials are talking about spending more money on repairing the roads next year. What's your opinion on that?

Citizen 1: The way I see it, the city should spend money on improving public transportation before fixing the potholes. I tend to think that people should drive less, and they can't do that without good public transportation.

News announcer: One of your fellow citizens believes that the city should spend more money on public transportation rather than on the roads next year. What are your thoughts on that issue?

Citizen 2: I wonder if we should spend any money on roads or transportation at all next year. It seems to me that the city's biggest problem right now is crime.

B PAIR WORK Practice the conversation.

CD2 42 **C** Listen. Write the three extra sentences you hear in the conversation. Practice the new conversation.

3 | Language Booster

A **Notice the ways we ask for opinions about issues and politely give opinions.**

Asking for opinions about issues	Politely giving opinions	
What's your opinion (on that)? What are your thoughts on that issue? How do you see the situation?	The way I see it I wonder if As I see it I tend to think that It seems to me that	the city should spend more money on education.

B **PAIR WORK** **Share your opinions about the issues in the Vocabulary section.**

Examples:

A: It seems to me that the city should try to reduce crime in the downtown area. I tend to think that the city should hire more police.

B: I tend to think that more police won't solve the problem. I wonder if crime would go down if businesses downtown didn't stay open late…

4 | Pronunciation Stress in two-syllable verbs

CD2 43 **A** **Listen to these sentences. Notice that two-syllable verbs often receive stress on the second syllable.**

1. We need to **reduce** crime in the city.
2. We have to in**crease** the budget for public transportation.
3. The city should im**prove** the school buildings.
4. Let's re**pair** the roads.

B **GROUP WORK** **Discuss the issues in Vocabulary section. This time, pay attention to the stress on two-syllable verbs.**

ONLINE PRACTICE

SPEAK *with* CONFIDENCE

A **PAIR WORK** **Write down three world issues that are important to you.**

Three important issues
1.
2.
3.

B **GROUP WORK** **Work in a group of three. Share opinions about one of the issues you listed above.**

English in Action

ONLINE PRACTICE

1 | Preview

PAIR WORK **Tom, Maria, and Alex are watching the news on TV. What do you think they're watching in each photo? Match. Explain your choices.**

a. a crime story	b. a sports story	c. a commercial	d. a political story

1

2

3

4

2 | Practice

A Watch the video. Complete the sentences with the correct answers.

1. The government reduced the budget for ____.
2. The score of the soccer game was probably ____.
3. Maria's favorite commercial is for ____.
4. The witness got a million dollars from ____.
5. Kate is going to ____.

B Watch the video again. Check your answers with a partner.

3 | Discuss

GROUP WORK **Answer the questions.**

1. If you were Kate, how would you spend the million-dollar reward?
2. Do you ever watch the news on TV? What parts do you like best? Least?
3. What's the most interesting news you heard? Why?

CONFIDENCE BOOSTER Student A: Turn to page 89.
Student B: Turn to page 97.

29 Did you see the game?

Student A and Student B: Take turns describing an event to your partner. Use the information below or think of your own ideas.

Your favorite sports team lost in a close game.

You went to see an Olympic event, and your favorite athlete lost when another athlete cheated.

I can talk about sporting events.
☐ Very well ☐ I need more practice.

I can change the subject.
☐ Very well ☐ I need more practice.

See Language Booster page 73.

30 Hold on.

Student A and Student B: Take turns telling each other about the news stories described below.

A man broke into store and the clerk was a former police officer.

A man stole $20 dollars from a woman's car, but the woman found the man's wallet in her car.

I can interrupt to ask for clarification.
☐ Very well ☐ I need more practice.

I can clarify.
☐ Very well ☐ I need more practice.

See Language Booster page 75.

31 Studies have shown...

Student A and Student B: Take turns describing the effectiveness of the following elements of advertising.

advertising jingles | slogans | television commercials | radio ads

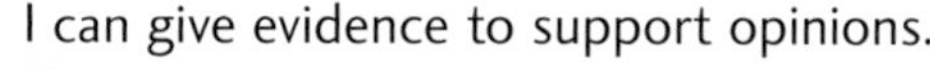

I can give evidence to support opinions.
☐ Very well ☐ I need more practice.

I can give examples to support opinions.
☐ Very well ☐ I need more practice.

See Language Booster page 77.

32 What's your opinion?

A Student A and Student B: Take turns asking for and sharing opinions on the issues below.

heavy traffic during rush hour | air pollution in the city | increasing food prices

B Now change roles. Student B gives a presentation and Student A asks follow-up questions.

I can ask for opinions about issues.
☐ Very well ☐ I need more practice.

I can politely give opinions.
☐ Very well ☐ I need more practice.

See Language Booster page 79.

1–4

Student A

What should I do?

1a. Read Tim's story. Ask Student B questions to fill in the blanks.

Example:

A: What did Tim get into recently?

B: Chess. What did he join?

A: He joined an online chess forum.

I recently got into ___chess___, so I joined an online chess forum. I played some good online games with ______________, and we sometimes chatted, too. We seemed to have lots of other things in common. For example, we both like action movies and ______________. So we decided to get together in person. Well, we met at ______________ and played some chess, then had lunch. We had a close chess game as usual. However, then the trouble started. The guy ______________ constantly! Every time I try to say something, he interrupts. I can't stand it when people interrupt me. So anyway, he's been ______________ a few times a day, wanting to get together again. He's really pushy. I don't want to be friends with him anymore, but I also don't want to ______________. What should I do?

1b. What do you think Tim should do? Discuss your ideas with Student B.

Conversation Practice

2. Have a conversation with Student B (1–8). Read the first sentence to him or her. Listen to Student B's response (2). If it is correct, choose the next correct response to continue the conversation.

1. So, I hear that you've had some bad luck lately.

3. a. Really? What happened?
   b. Why did you decide to do that?

5. a. Oh, I can't stand when people do that. How did you react?
   b. Oh, so it sounds like you got a lucky break.

7. a. You might want to think about getting your car fixed at Hill's Service Station. They do great work.
   b. Oh, well that's good. So, did you confront the other driver?

CONFIDENCE BOOSTER 1–4

pair with Student B CONFIDENCE BOOSTER 1–4 on p. 90

5–8

Student A
Has she changed?

1a. You went to your high school reunion last weekend. Tell Student B about the people you talked to. Complete the chart.

Example:

A: Who did you talk to at the reunion?
B: Let's see…I talked to Teresa Perez.
A: That name sounds familiar. Who is she, again?
B: She's my old roommate.
A: Oh, that's right. Has she changed much?
B: Oh, yes. She used to be on the quiet side, but now she's bubbly

Name	His/Her relationship to you	What he/she used to be like	What he/she is like now
Teresa Perez	*old roommate*		
Kevin Johnson	old soccer teammate	serious	witty
Elizabeth Morris			
Mrs. Keating	former professor	unapproachable	friendly
John Nolting			
Brad Chen	sister's ex-boyfriend	insecure	self-confident

1b. Do you know someone who has changed? Tell Student B about the person. Answer these questions.

1. What is his/her name?
2. How do you know the person?
3. What did the person use to be like?
4. What is the person like now?

Conversation Practice

2. Have a conversation with Student B (1–8). Read the first sentence to him or her. Listen to Student B's response (2). If it is correct, choose the next correct response to continue the conversation.

1. A bunch of us are going to a free jazz concert in the park tonight. Daniel posted something about it on Facebook. Do you feel like joining us?

3. a. Sure, I can pick you up. I'll come by around 7:00.
   b. So you have to study a lot, huh? Couldn't you study tomorrow instead?

5. a. You're right. Jazz does have a really good beat.
   b. Well, you know, until recently I'd assumed I wouldn't like jazz either.

7. a. Well, my brother took me to a few great concerts, and now I love it! You should give it a try.
   b. Well, it's just not my thing.

CONFIDENCE BOOSTER 5–8

9–12

Student A
Lifestyle changes

1a. People are going to make changes to their lifestyles. Ask and answer questions to complete the chart.

Example:

A: What is Ted's problem?

B: He's always tired.

A: How is he going to change his lifestyle?

Name	Problem	Lifestyle change	Benefit
Ted	is always tired		
Abby	has an unhealthy diet	eat less junk food and more fruits and vegetables	feel healthier
Sylvia			
Nick	has a very cluttered apartment	tidy up for 15 minutes every evening	have a neater apartment
Peter			
Clara	is out of shape	exercise every day	get in shape

1b. Which of the problems in the chart do you have? How could you change your lifestyle to solve the problems? Discuss your ideas with Student B.

Example:

A: I'm out of shape because I don't get enough exercise. I could go for a run every evening.

B: I am always tired. I should go to bed earlier every night. I would have more energy.

Conversation Practice

2. Have a conversation with Student B (1–8). Read the first sentence to him or her. Listen to Student B's response (2). If it is correct, choose the next correct response to continue the conversation.

1. Wow, you're up early!

3. a. Really? Good for you! What kind of exercise are you going to do?
   b. Really? Why are you going to work an hour earlier than usual?

5. a. Yes, I'd love a ride to class. Thanks.
   b. Oh. What exactly is tai chi, anyway?

7. a. My favorite kind of exercise is yoga. Don't you think it's relaxing?
   b. It sounds fun, but I don't like to get up early. Don't you think sleep is just as important as exercise?

pair with Student B CONFIDENCE BOOSTER 9–12 on p. 92

13–16

Student A
Seeking a tour guide

1a. Joe and Katrina both interviewed for the position below. Read the job description. Then ask and answer questions to complete the chart.

Job description: We are seeking a tour guide to join our dynamic company. The tour guide will be responsible for guiding week-long bus tours for international tour groups. The ideal candidate must be energetic, organized, and have excellent communication skills. Fluency in English and Spanish is essential; more languages are a plus! A high school diploma is required, but a college degree is preferred.

	Joe	Katrina
Experience	6 months – receptionist at a travel agency	1 year – gave city walking tours
Education		College degree; tourism major
Languages		Fluent in Spanish and English; also speaks some French
Long-term goals		Manage an international hotel
Strengths		Organized, responsible, a team player, a hard worker
Weaknesses		Didn't make much eye contact during the interview

1b. Who would you hire for the job, Joe or Katrina? Why? Discuss your ideas with Student B.

Conversation Practice

2. Have a conversation with Student B (1–8). Read the first sentence to him or her. Listen to Student B's response (2). If it is correct, choose the next correct response to continue the conversation.

1. So tell me, what would you bring to our organization?

3. a. Oh, that's good. Could you say a bit more about your strengths?
   b. Keep in mind that we are looking for someone with a lot of experience.

5. a. So what you're saying is that you're a hard worker. OK, could you tell me why you left your previous job?
   b. I see. So it sounds like you're good with people. OK, could you tell me about the biggest challenge you've ever faced at work?

7. a. Wow! That's impressive. So, do you have any questions about our company or the job?
   b. It sounds like you had a great weekend.

17–20

Student A

What are you afraid of?

1a. **Read the questions. Write your answers under *You* in the chart.**

Name	Natalie	Sam	You	Student B
What are you afraid of?		spiders		
What causes you stress?	being overworked			
What would you do if you could do anything?		invent a flying car		
What do you regret?	not taking more science classes			

1b. **Ask and answer questions to complete the chart. First ask about Natalie and Sam, and then ask about Student B.**

Example:

A: What is Natalie afraid of?

B: She's afraid of heights. What is Sam afraid of?

A: He's afraid of spiders.

Conversation Practice

2. **Have a conversation with Student B (1–8). Read the first sentence to him or her. Listen to Student B's response (2). If it is correct, choose the next correct response to continue the conversation.**

1. I never should have agreed to go to Australia with my sister.

3. a. Well, for one thing, I'm really afraid of flying. I usually drive or take the train.
   b. Because I've always wanted to learn to surf.

5. a. That's a good idea. But the other reason I'm stressed about the trip is that I'm really overworked at the moment.
   b. Really? I like staying up late, too. But I have an early morning flight.

7. a. Yes, I'm really afraid of missing my flight. I'm planning to get to the airport very early.
   b. Not really…I'm just nervous about having a huge amount of work when I get back.

Student A
The year's best

1a. Ask and answer questions to complete the article.

Example:

A: What was the most popular movie of the year?

B: It was *Seeing Only Good.*

A: Oh, what's it about?

The Year in Review

We asked you, our readers, to give us your opinions of the year's best movie, music, and celebrity news. Here's what you told us:

The Best Movie

The most popular movie of the year was the hit ______________________. This science fiction hit starring ______________________ takes place in the year 2084, and tells the story of a city where ______________________. They can only become visible again by doing good things. Our readers thought it was a ______________________ movie. If you haven't seen it, you should!

The Best Music

Readers voted on Marly Santora's new release *Freddo* as the best album of the year. They love the music's ______________________. The lyrics are provocative yet hilarious, and tell the story of ______________________. Even the title has a sense of humor–though it means "cold and passionless" in Italian, Marly's music is quite the opposite!

Celebrity Gossip

There wasn't any disagreement about this year's juiciest celebrity news – it was definitely Owen and

1b. What do you think was last year's best movie? Best album? Share your ideas with Student B.

Conversation Practice

2a. Have a conversation with Student B (1–8). Read the first sentence to him or her. Listen to Student B's response (2). If it is correct, choose the next correct response to continue the conversation.

1. Have you heard the latest celebrity gossip? Adrianna and Vince just bought two houses!

3. a. Yeah, Adrianna just broke up with Matt Morgan last year, and she's marrying Vince in September.
   b. Yeah, so now they have seven. And get this—Adrianna just started filming a new movie, too.

5. a. Ryan Wallace is starring in it with her. He's such a great actor, isn't he?
   b. Actually, I think it's a thriller. It's about this woman who…

7. a. Yeah, I always watch the Academy Awards. Don't you think her acceptance speech was a little too long?
   b. Yeah, I did. Her dress was pretty wild, wasn't it? I suppose she's a trendsetter, but if you ask me, she looked kind of ridiculous.

25–28 Student A

How was your stay?

1a. Ask and answers questions about Jake's vacation to complete his travel survey.

Example:

A: Where did Jake go?

B: He went to Peru. Where did he stay?

A: He stayed at a…

Thank you for booking your trip through TripPlanners International. We welcome your feedback so that we can make your next vacation even better!

Where did you go?

Where did you stay?
☐ bed and breakfast ☐ hostel ☐ luxury hotel ☒ budget hotel

How was your stay?
☐ Excellent ☐ Good ☐ OK ☐ Bad

What airline did you fly on? Clear Skies

How was your flight experience?
☐ Excellent ☐ Very good ☐ OK ☐ Bad

Did you have any travel problems?
1) My flight to Lima was delayed by two hours.
2)
3) My hotel was a little noisy sometimes.

How did you sightsee?
☐ took a guided tour ☐ explored on my own

Do you have any tips for traveling to this destination?
1)
2) Go there during the dry season.

end of survey

1b. Think of a trip you have taken. Ask and answer the questions above with Student B.

Conversation Practice

2. Have a conversation with Student B (1–8). Read the first sentence to him or her. Listen to Student B's response (2). If it is correct, choose the next correct response to continue the conversation.

1. I can't wait for our trip to Thailand. We should start planning the details, shouldn't we?

3. a. We should probably make reservations…We're going during the peak tourist season, right?
   b. Oh, thanks so much for making the reservations.

5. a. Well, I'd like to splurge, but I'm afraid I can't afford it.
   b. Yes, we should definitely stay in a hostel.

7. a. Yes, I've made a long list of all the places I want to visit in Thailand.
   b. No, not yet. Be sure to bring some long pants. I've heard it's inappropriate to wear shorts when you visit temples.

pair with Student B CONFIDENCE BOOSTER 25–28 *on p. 96*

Student A
Who won the game?

1a. Read the news stories. Ask and answer questions to find the differences between your stories and Student B's stories. Do NOT read your story to Student B!

Example:

A: Who won the game between Brazil and Argentina?

B: Argentina won.

A: Oh. According to my story, Brazil won.

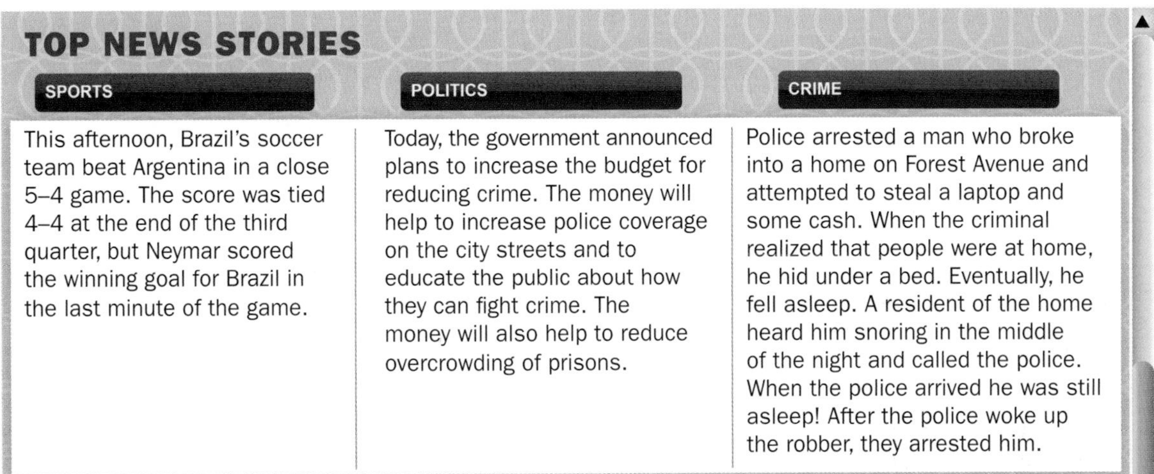

TOP NEWS STORIES

SPORTS

This afternoon, Brazil's soccer team beat Argentina in a close 5–4 game. The score was tied 4–4 at the end of the third quarter, but Neymar scored the winning goal for Brazil in the last minute of the game.

POLITICS

Today, the government announced plans to increase the budget for reducing crime. The money will help to increase police coverage on the city streets and to educate the public about how they can fight crime. The money will also help to reduce overcrowding of prisons.

CRIME

Police arrested a man who broke into a home on Forest Avenue and attempted to steal a laptop and some cash. When the criminal realized that people were at home, he hid under a bed. Eventually, he fell asleep. A resident of the home heard him snoring in the middle of the night and called the police. When the police arrived he was still asleep! After the police woke up the robber, they arrested him.

1b. Close your book and try to retell the stories to Student B.

Conversation Practice

2. Have a conversation with Student B (1–8). Read the first sentence to him or her. Listen to Student B's response (2). If it is correct, choose the next correct response to continue the conversation.

1. The government is spending way too much money these days. For instance, did you hear that they approved a budget increase to repair and expand the soccer stadium?

3. a. Well, I wonder if the city should spend money on that. Isn't the stadium big enough already?
   b. I agree. I don't think the city should increase spending right now.

5. a. Hold on. Did you say the stream near the city might flood?
   b. Wait, what did you say about the city's…something stream?

7. a. How do you see the situation?
   b. Huh. As I see it, the soccer club will make more money, not the city.

1–4

Student B

What should I do?

1a. Read Tim's story. Ask Student A questions to fill in the blanks.

Example:

A: What did Tim get into recently?

B: Chess. What did he join?

A: He joined an online chess forum.

I recently got into chess, so I joined an online _chess forum_. I played some good online games with a guy named Matt, and we sometimes ______________, too. We seemed to have lots of other things in common. For example, we both like ______________ and comic books. So we decided to ______________. Well, we met at a cafe and played some chess, then had lunch. We had a ______________ chess game as usual. However, then the trouble started. The guy talks constantly! Every time I try to say something, he ______________. I can't stand it when people interrupt me. So anyway, he's been texting and calling me a few times a day, wanting to get together again. He's really ______________. I don't want to be friends with him anymore, but I also don't want to hurt his feelings.

1b. What do you think Tim should do? Discuss your ideas with a Student A.

Conversation Practice

2. Have a conversation with Student A (1–8). Listen to his or her sentence. Read the sentences in (2) and choose the correct response. Listen to Student A's response (3). If it is correct, choose the next correct response to continue the conversation.

2. a. Yeah, that's for sure. I got into an accident last weekend.
   b. Yeah, I've been working really hard this week.

4. a. That really gets on my nerves.
   b. Well, I was driving home from work, and the car behind me was tailgating.

6. a. Well, I was annoyed, but I didn't do anything. Anyway, a cat ran out in front of my car, so I stopped suddenly, and the car behind me hit me. Fortunately, no one got injured, and our cars weren't damaged.
   b. I'm not sure. I was walking down the street when I fell and hit my head.

8. a. Actually, no. I didn't feel comfortable doing that. He was my boss!
   b. Yes, I learned a lot from this experience.

pair with Student A CONFIDENCE BOOSTER 1–4 on p. 82

5–8

Student B

Has she changed?

1a. You went to your high school reunion last weekend. Tell Student A about the people you talked to. Complete the chart.

Example:

A: Who did you talk to at the reunion?
B: Let's see…I talked to Teresa Perez.
A: That name sounds familiar.
Who is she, again?
B: She's my old roommate.
A: Oh, that's right. Has she changed much?
B: Oh, yes. She used to be on the quiet side, but now she's bubbly

Name	His/Her relationship to you	What he/she used to be like	What he/she is like now
Teresa Perez	old roommate	on the quiet side	bubbly
Kevin Johnson			
Elizabeth Morris	old tennis buddy	sweet	sarcastic
Mrs. Keating			
John Nolting	acquaintance from English class	shy	gregarious
Brad Chen			

1b. Do you know someone who has changed? Tell Student A about the person. Answer these questions.

1. What is his or her name?
2. How do you know the person?
3. What did the person use to be like?
4. What is the person like now?

Conversation Practice

2. Have a conversation with Student A (1–8). Listen to his or her sentence. Read the sentences in (2) and choose the correct response. Listen to Student A's response (3). If it is correct, choose the next correct response to continue the conversation..

2. a. Oh, thanks, but I'm not sure I'm up for that tonight. I have a big exam this week.
   b. Oh, I love Facebook, too. I have over 500 friends.

4. a. Actually, I'm pretty beat. And jazz just doesn't really interest me. I just don't get why you like it so much.
   b. I'm studying Chinese history. It's really interesting.

6. a. I know what you mean. I don't like it, either.
   b. Really? So how did you get into it?

8. a. Well, maybe some other time. But tonight I really do need to study.
   b. Your brother sounds really extroverted.

9–12

Student B
Lifestyle changes

1a. People are going to make changes to their lifestyles. Ask and answer questions to complete the chart.

Example:

A: What is Ted's problem?

B: He's always tired.

A: How is he going to change his lifestyle?

Name	Problem	Lifestyle change	Benefit
Ted	is always tired	go to bed an hour earlier every night	have more energy
Abby			
Sylvia	is often late to work	get up half an hour earlier every morning	get to work on time
Nick			
Peter	isn't very environmentally responsible	bike to work instead of drive	reduce his carbon footprint
Clara			

1b. Which of the problems in the chart do you have? How could you change your lifestyle to solve the problems? Discuss your ideas with Student A.

Example:

A: I'm out of shape because I don't get enough exercise. I could go for a run every evening.

B: I am always tired. I should go to bed earlier every night. I would have more energy.

Conversation Practice

2. Have a conversation with Student A (1–8). Listen to his or her sentence. Read the sentences in (2) and choose the correct response. Listen to Student A's response (3). If it is correct, choose the next correct response to continue the conversation.

2. a. Because I wasn't tired.
   b. Yeah, I decided to get up an hour earlier every morning, so I can exercise before work.

4. a. I'm going to take a tai chi class.
   b. I'm going to do that grammar exercise.

6. a. It's a kind of exercise that uses slow, relaxed movements. You should join me!
   b. Tai chi is really hard, but I like it anyway.

8. a. I didn't get enough sleep last night, either.
   b. You have a point, but I still think you'd really enjoy tai chi!

pair with Student A CONFIDENCE BOOSTER 9–12 *on p. 84*

Student B

Seeking a tour guide

1a. Joe and Katrina both interviewed for the position below. Read the job description. Then ask and answer questions to complete the chart.

Job description: We are seeking a tour guide to join our dynamic company. The tour guide will be responsible for guiding week-long bus tours for international tour groups. The ideal candidate must be energetic, organized, and have excellent communication skills. Fluency in English and Spanish is essential; more languages are a plus! A high school diploma is required, but a college degree is preferred.

	Joe	Katrina
Experience	6 months – receptionist at a travel agency	1 year – gave city walking tours
Education	High school diploma	
Languages	Fluent in English, Spanish, Portuguese, and Mandarin Chinese	
Long-term goals	Travel to as many countries as possible	
Strengths	Energetic, gregarious, excellent communication skills, very positive attitude	
Weaknesses	May be somewhat disorganized; arrived ten minutes late for the interview	

1b. Who would you hire for the job, Joe or Katrina? Why? Discuss your ideas with Student A.

Conversation Practice

2. Have a conversation with Student A (1–8). Listen to his or her sentence. Read the sentences in (2) and choose the correct response. Listen to Student A's response (3). If it is correct, choose the next correct response to continue the conversation.

2. a. Well, my long-term goal is to own a restaurant.
   b. Well, I'm very detail oriented, I'm a hard worker, and I have a lot of experience in this field.

4. a. Let me see. I'm good at motivating people, and I have good communication skills.
   b. I hope to get a position as a customer service representative.

6. a. That's an interesting question. I would have to say it was the time that I had to prepare a 25-page report in one weekend.
   b. Let me think. I guess it was the time I won the employee-of-the-month award.

8. a. Yes. I have a college degree, and I majored in economics.
   b. Yes. You mentioned that the job would involve travel. Could you tell me a little more about that?

pair with **Student A** CONFIDENCE BOOSTER 13–16 *on p. 85*

17–20

Student B

What are you afraid of?

1a. Read the questions. Write your answers under *You* in the chart.

Name	Natalie	Sam	You	Student B
What are you afraid of?	heights			
What causes you stress?		taking tests		
What would you do if you could do anything?	discover a new planet			
What do you regret?		spending so much money last summer		

1b. Ask and answer questions to complete the chart. First ask about Natalie and Sam, and ask about Student A.

Example:

A: What is Natalie afraid of?

B: She's afraid of heights. What is Sam afraid of?

A: He's afraid of spiders.

Conversation Practice

2. Have a conversation with Student A (1–8). Listen to his or her sentence. Read the sentences in (2) and choose the correct response. Listen to Student A's response (3). If it is correct, choose the next correct response to continue the conversation.

2. a. Oh, really? Why is that?
   b. Oh, that's great! You must be really excited.

4. a. Well, it's cheaper to take the train than to drive. Gas is really expensive these days.
   b. Oh, is that right? I am, too. I find it's helpful to stay up really late the night before, so I can sleep on the plane.

6. a. Oh, so do you wish you were taking more time off?
   b. Oh, so are you afraid of missing deadlines?

8. a. Well, be sure to pack light so you don't hurt your back when you lift your suitcase.
   b. Well, in my experience, you forget about work as soon as you're on vacation. Just go and have fun, and worry about work when you get back!

pair with Student A CONFIDENCE BOOSTER 17–20 on p. 86

Student B
The year's best

1a. Ask and answer questions to complete the article.

Example:

A: What was the most popular movie of the year?

B: It was *Seeing Only Good.*

A: Oh, what's it about?

The Year in Review

We asked you, our readers, to give us your opinions of the year's best movie, music, and celebrity news. Here's what you told us:

The Best Movie

The most popular movie of the year was the hit *Seeing Only Good*. This ______________ hit starring Amelia Morrissey and Zeke Zaffron takes place in the year ______________, and tells the story of a city where people who do bad things become invisible. They can only become visible again by ______________. Our readers thought it was a heartwarming, feel-good movie. If you haven't seen it, you should!

The Best Music

Readers voted on Marly Santora's new release ______________ as the best album of the year. They love the music's great beat and danceable tunes. The lyrics are provocative yet ______________, and tell the story of Marly's life. Even the title has a sense a humor—though it means ______________ in Italian, Marly's music is quite the opposite!

Celebrity Gossip

There wasn't any disagreement about this year's juiciest celebrity news—it was definitely Owen and

1b. 1b. What do you think was last year's best movie? Best album? Share your ideas with Student A.

Conversation Practice

2a. Have a conversation with Student A (1–8). Listen to his or her sentence. Read the sentences in (2) and choose the correct response. Listen to Student A's response (3). If it is correct, choose the next correct response to continue the conversation.

2. a. You can't be serious! Don't they already have three houses?
   b. You're kidding! I thought they'd stay together forever!

4. a. Really? Is it another corny romance?
   b. Really? Have you seen it yet?

6. a. Wait! Don't tell me! I want to be surprised. Anyway, did you see her at the Academy Awards last week? What did you think of that dress?
   b. Oh, I'm definitely going to see it. I love romances. And Ryan Wallace is amazing.

8. a. Yeah, I know what you mean. But I'm not exactly up on the current styles.
   b. Yeah, her dress must have cost thousands of dollars.

25–28

CONFIDENCE BOOSTER 25–28

Student B

How was your stay?

1a. **Ask and answers questions about Jake's vacation to complete his travel survey.**

Example:

A: Where did Jake go?

B: He went to Peru. Where did he stay?

A: He stayed at a…

Thank you for booking your trip through TripPlanners International. We welcome your feedback so that we can make your next vacation even better!

Where did you go? Peru

Where did you stay?
☐ bed and breakfast ☐ hostel ☐ luxury hotel ☐ budget hotel

How was your stay?
☐ Excellent ☒ Good ☐ OK ☐ Bad

What airline did you fly on?

How was your flight experience?
☐ Excellent ☒ Very good ☐ OK ☐ Bad

Did you have any travel problems?
1)
2) My luggage was misplaced, and the airline delivered it the next day.
3)

How did you sightsee?
☒ took a guided tour ☐ explored on my own

Do you have any tips for traveling to this destination?
1) Try to meet some Peruvian people. They are warm and friendly!
2)

end of survey

1b. **Think of a trip you have taken. Ask and answer the questions above with Student A.**

Conversation Practice

2. **Have a conversation with Student A (1–8). Listen to his or her sentence. Read the sentences in (2) and choose the correct response. Listen to Student A's response (3). If it is correct, choose the next correct response to continue the conversation.**

2. a. I can't wait, either. I hope we have nice weather.
   b. Yeah, definitely. Should we make reservations in advance?

4. a. That's right. Should we stay in a hostel? Or should we splurge and stay in a nice hotel?
   b. That's right. There won't be many tourists at that time of year.

6. a. I agree that we should splurge. After all, it is a vacation.
   b. Good point. I really can't either. So, have you made a packing list yet?

8. a. Oh, OK. I usually only wear jeans.
   b. OK. I'll be sure to pack lots of shorts. It's going to be hot there.

pair with Student A CONFIDENCE BOOSTER 25–28 on p. 88

Student B

Who won the game?

1a. Read the news stories. Ask and answer questions to find the differences between your stories and Student A's stories. Do NOT read your story to Student A!

Example:

A: Who won the game between Brazil and Argentina?

B: Argentina won.

A: Oh. According to my story, Brazil won.

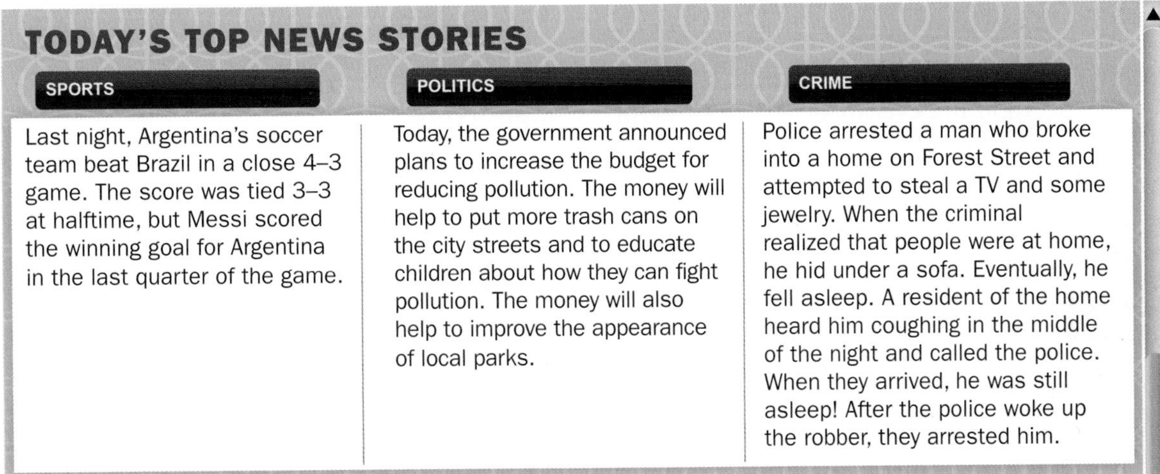

TODAY'S TOP NEWS STORIES

SPORTS	POLITICS	CRIME
Last night, Argentina's soccer team beat Brazil in a close 4–3 game. The score was tied 3–3 at halftime, but Messi scored the winning goal for Argentina in the last quarter of the game.	Today, the government announced plans to increase the budget for reducing pollution. The money will help to put more trash cans on the city streets and to educate children about how they can fight pollution. The money will also help to improve the appearance of local parks.	Police arrested a man who broke into a home on Forest Street and attempted to steal a TV and some jewelry. When the criminal realized that people were at home, he hid under a sofa. Eventually, he fell asleep. A resident of the home heard him coughing in the middle of the night and called the police. When they arrived, he was still asleep! After the police woke up the robber, they arrested him.

1b. Close your book and try to retell the stories to Student A.

Conversation Practice

2. Have a conversation with Student A (1–8). Listen to his or her sentence. Read the sentences in (2) and choose the correct response. Listen to Student A's response (3). If it is correct, choose the next correct response to continue the conversation.

2. a. Really? I tend to think that's a good idea, actually.
   b. Oh, that's too bad. I'm a big soccer fan.

4. a. I've heard that the stadium holds about 70,000 fans.
   b. You know, studies have shown that if they build a bigger stadium, they can sell more tickets and increase the city's revenue stream.

6. a. Revenue stream. That means the city will make more money.
   b. I said that the city is going provide streaming video of all of its meetings.

8. a. Yeah, wouldn't it be great if the city made more money?
   b. Actually, they'll both make more money. The more successful businesses are, the more taxes they'll have to pay to the city.

Audio and Video Scripts

LESSON 1

Listening, Part A and B

1. Alex: Hi, Clara. I hear you made a change recently.

Clara: Oh, hi, Alex. Yeah, I did. I took a risk and made the decision to go back to school.

Alex: Oh, wow! That's amazing, Clara. What are you studying?

Clara: I'm studying to be a teacher.

Alex: I think you'd be a wonderful teacher, Clara.

Clara: Thanks, Alex. I think it's the best decision I've ever made. So, how about you? What have you been up to?

Alex: Me? Well, I faced a challenge last year, and I lost my job. Half of the employees at my company got laid off.

Clara: Oh, no! That's a shame. You're in sales, right?

Alex: Yes, that's right. Being unemployed for a year was one of the biggest challenges I've ever faced. But I had a great opportunity last week. I ran into an old friend, and he offered me a job at his company. I start on Monday.

Clara: That's great! Congratulations!

2. Larissa: Hey, Victor. How are you?

Victor: Hi, Larissa. I'm doing well, thanks.

Larissa: I'm surprised to see you at a bakery in the middle of the afternoon. You're usually at the office in the afternoons, aren't you?

Victor: Well, I decided to take a risk and start my own business.

Larissa: Oh, wow! That's really brave of you.

Victor: It was scary, but starting my own business is one of the most exciting things I've ever done.

Larissa: What is your new business?

Victor: This bakery! We just opened two weeks ago.

Larissa: Really? Congratulations! It's a really nice place.

Victor: Thanks, Larissa. I'm really happy with how it's going.

Larissa: How did you decide to open a bakery?

Victor: Well, I got into baking a couple of years ago, just for fun, but I ended up really enjoying it. Then a few months ago, I decided it was time for me to make a change. Oh, that reminds me, I hear that you just made a change, too.

Larissa: Yes, I did. I got married last month.

Victor: That's great! Congratulations! Let's have a piece of cake to celebrate.

Larissa: Thanks, I'd love to!

LESSON 2

Conversation, Part C

Adam: Hey, did you hear about the man who fell onto a subway track last week?

Teresa: No, how did that happen?

Adam: He was texting a friend, and he wasn't watching where he was going. He fell, hit his head, and passed out. He was just lying there, and a train was coming.

Teresa: No way. What happened next?

Adam: Luckily, someone witnessed the whole thing. He jumped onto the track and pulled the guy out. Someone else called the emergency services.

Teresa: Wow! Did the guy injure himself in the fall? People really shouldn't text while they're walking.

Adam: Not really. The guy woke up after a few minutes, and he was fine. He got up and finished typing his text message!

LESSON 3

Listening, Part A and B

1. A: I was just at the grocery story waiting in line, and the woman next to me just kept looking at me. It gets on my nerves when people stare at me.

B: That's so weird. I wonder why she was staring at you.

A: I have no idea. It was making me nervous. I kept thinking I had food on my face.

2. A: I'm getting so frustrated at work. One of my co-workers interrupts me when I'm talking. She does it all the time, especially in meetings. I can't stand it when people interrupt.
B: I can't either. That's so rude. Can you talk to her about it?
A: I have talked to her about it, but she says that she doesn't realize she's doing it. I don't know what to do.
B: The next time she interrupts you, just say, "I wasn't finished speaking."
A: I'll try that next time. I hope it works.

3. A: We've been sitting here for 30 minutes, waiting to try on these shoes, and no one is offering to help us. It drives me crazy when salespeople ignore me.
B: I could go ask one of them to help us.
A: No, let's see if they notice us. I would understand it if they were busy, but we're the only people in the store. And they're just chatting. One of them is on the phone with his friend.
B: I'm going to go over there and ask for help.
A: Good luck!

4. A: How did your date go?
B: It was awful. My date was texting someone the whole time. I hate it when people text while I'm talking to them.
A: I do, too! It's so rude. Do you know who he was texting?
B: I think he was texting his boss. I understand that his job is important, but it was ridiculous.
A: How did the date end?
B: He actually asked me if I wanted to have dinner next week!

LESSON 4

Conversation, Part C

Ingrid: Hi, Robert. Where's Pablo? I thought he was hanging out with us tonight.
Robert: Hi, Ingrid. He canceled at the last minute.
Ingrid: Again? You put up with a lot from him. He did this last time.
Robert: Yeah, he keeps doing it. I'm starting to resent him for it.
Ingrid: Have you tried confronting him about it? You should talk to him.
Robert: Do you really think that's a good idea? I don't want to be pushy and have an awkward conversation.
Ingrid: If you don't feel comfortable talking to him, you might want to consider texting him about it. And you can think about what you're going to write.
Robert: That's not a bad idea. I'll give it a try.
Ingrid: Great! Let me know how it turns out.

LESSONS 1–4 ENGLISH IN ACTION

Maria: Hi...Kate, right? I'm Maria.
Kate: Nice to meet you in person.
Maria: Come on in...take a look around.
Kate: Wow, this place is really nice! Big, and light...and so neat!
Maria: Yeah, I'm kind of a neatnik.
Kate: Oh, I know what you mean. I'm totally the same way.
Maria: Really?
Kate: Yeah, I just can't stand it when people leave their stuff all over the place, or, you know, leave dirty dishes in the sink.
Maria: That's great to hear! So, have a seat. Can I get you anything to drink?
Kate: Oh, no thanks. I stopped for coffee on the way here. So, how long have you been looking for a new roommate?
Maria: Oh, for a couple of weeks or so. I've talked to about five people, but no one has seemed quite right. So, in your profile you said you're new to the city, right?
Kate: Yeah, I lost my job a few months ago. I couldn't find another job near where I lived, so I decided to take a job in a different city. At first, I was pretty upset about losing my job, but then I got a lucky break. Losing my job was one of the biggest challenges I've ever faced, but it turned out to be the best thing that ever happened to me.
Maria: Well, that's great! I'm still looking for a job. I'm not really sure what I want to do...

Kate: I'm sure you'll figure it out.
Maria: Yeah. I hope so. So, did you live with roommates before, or your parents, or...
Kate: Yeah, I lived with a couple of roommates. I got along great with one of them. But the other...well...she was basically a nice person, but we were just really different.
Maria: Oh? In what way?
Kate: Well, like I said, I'm really neat, and she was pretty messy. And she was noisy... you know, she was always watching TV and talking on the phone and having her friends over. She just really got on my nerves.
Maria: Oh, no! I can't stand messy people. Did you hear about the woman who sued her roommate?
Kate: No. What happened?
Maria: Apparently, the woman had asked her roommate to clean up. She never did, and the house got so messy that the woman sued her roommate.
Kate: What a nightmare!
Maria: Yeah, I hear you. I'm lucky...my old roommate was wonderful. The only thing that bugged me about her was that she was always late.
Kate: Oh, I hate it when people are late! I always try to be on time. A lot of times I arrive at places early, actually.
Maria: So, it sounds like we're the perfect match! When can you move in?

[Later that day...]
Maria: OK, so Tom, you're not going to believe this...
Tom: What happened?
Maria: Well I just got home, and Kate's not here, and...well, just take a look at this.
Tom: Wow. Oh, no.
Maria: Yeah! Kate said she was really neat! What am I going to do?
Tom: Well, uh, you might want to consider the direct approach. You know, just confront her about it when she gets home.
Maria: I don't know...do you really think that's a good idea? I mean, she just moved in. I'm not sure how she'd react...it could be pretty awkward.

LESSON 5

Conversation, Part C

Luisa: So, how do you know Eva?
Sarah: Well, Eva's my old neighbor. I used to live in the apartment across from hers. I lived there for about five years.
Luisa: Oh, right. I think we've met before.
Sarah: Yes, you look familiar. You used to come over to visit Eva once in a while.
Luisa: That's right. Eva is a former classmate of mine. We had a few classes together in college, and we used to study together a lot.
Sarah: I see. And what do you do now?
Luisa: I work as an assistant in an advertising firm. We do a lot of car advertisements.
Sarah: That sounds interesting. Do you enjoy it?
Luisa: Yes, I do. It's a great job.

LESSON 6

Listening, Part A and B

1. A: Hi, Ellen. How are you?
B: Hi, Daniel. I'm great! What's up?
A: I was just wondering…do you feel like listening to live music tonight? I have an extra ticket to the symphony.
B: That sounds really fun, but I'm afraid I have other plans. I'm going to see a movie with Tina tonight.
A: Oh, what movie are you seeing?
B: We're going to see *Night of the Lake Creature*.
A: Oh, I heard that's really scary. Have a great time!
B: Thanks. Enjoy the concert!

2. A: Hey, are you up for catching a movie tonight?
B: I'm not sure I'm up for that tonight. I'm pretty beat.
A: Oh, why are you so tired?
B: Well, I had three classes today, and I had to work for four hours afterward.
A: Wow, yeah, you must be exhausted. Well, how about tomorrow night?
B: Yeah, tomorrow night sounds good. I have the whole day off tomorrow.
A: Great! Let's meet at the theater at 7:00.
B: Sounds good. See you then!

3. A: What do you think about going to Ken's house with me tonight? We're going to play video games.
   B: Oh, does he have that new game he was going to get?
   A: Yeah, he bought it yesterday.
   B: I really wish I could, but I have to work tonight.
   A: That's too bad. What time do you get off work?
   B: I work until 10:00. Will you still be playing then?
   A: Probably. Last time we played until 2:00 in the morning.
   B: All right. Maybe I can swing by after work.

4. A: Hi, Maria. What do you say we try out the new restaurant down the street tonight? I've heard it's really good.
   B: Hey, Kim, I'm not sure I'm up for that tonight. I don't really feel well.
   A: Oh, no! What's wrong? Are you sick?
   B: Yeah, I think I have a cold.
   A: Do you have a fever?
   B: No, no fever. I just have a headache and a stuffy nose. And I'm kind of achy.
   A: That's terrible. I'll bring you some chicken soup.
   B: You don't have to do that.
   A: It's really no problem. I'll see you in half an hour.
   B: Thanks, Kim. That's really sweet of you.

LESSON 7

Conversation, Part C

Anna: Do you know Susan Park?
Crystal: Yeah, I know her. We had a few classes together last semester. Why do you ask?
Anna: I don't think she likes me. She seems kind of conceited. She never talks to me.
Crystal: Oh, I'm sure she likes you. I used to think she didn't like me, too.
Anna: Really?
Crystal: Yeah. I had thought she was standoffish, but it turns out she is actually just introverted. She's on the quiet side, but she's very witty.
Anna: So what you're saying is, you really like her.
Crystal: Yeah, I do. Once she felt comfortable with me, she opened up. We get along great now.
Anna: That's good to know. I'll try a little harder to talk to her.

LESSON 8

Listening, Part A and B

A: What are you doing, Ben?
B: I'm looking at posts on Pinterest.
A: Oh, I've never used Pinterest. I saw it once, and I don't think it's very interesting.
B: I just don't get why you don't like it. There's a lot of great stuff on here! And I can keep track of all the things I'm interested in and share it with others. I didn't know I had so many interests until I started Pinterest!
A: I can see why some people like it, but it's not for me. I'd rather just go on Facebook.
B: People post interesting things on Facebook, too, but Pinterest has great photos and things to look at. Plus, I'm an artist, and looking at Pinterest gives me a lot of ideas. You should give it another try.
A: I'll think about it. Do you use Twitter?
B: No. Do you?
A: Yes! I love Twitter!
B: What do you like about it?
A: I can connect with thousands of people around the world who share the same interests. I get most of my information and news updates from Twitter. Why don't you use it?
B: People who use Twitter are on it all day!
A: What do you mean?
B: You. You've been on your phone the whole time we've been talking. You're on your phone tweeting.
A: I just have to retweet something. Sorry. I'll lose followers if I don't post or connect with other tweeters!
B: I don't think it matters, does it? Unless you want to lose a real friend.
A: OK! OK! I'm done!

LESSON 5–8 ENGLISH IN ACTION

Tom: Hey, Alex. My friend Anna just opened a cafe and is having a little get-together there. How about joining me?

Alex: Huh? Oh, I'm not really in the mood to go out tonight. I think I'll just stay in and read or something.

Tom: Are you sure? I just don't get why you'd want to stay home all alone.

Alex: Come on, you know me...I'm kind of a homebody.

Tom: Give me a break, Alex. You're no homebody. It's Anna, isn't it? You don't really like her, right?

Alex: Oh...well...she's smart, and creative, and everything...but she just seems kind of...I don't know...mean.

Tom: Oh, yeah, I used to think that, too. But then I realized that she's just really sarcastic. And you know, sometimes she can actually be kind of sweet.

Alex: Maybe I should get to know her better. But not tonight...I'm pretty beat...

Tom: OK. Well, swing by if you change your mind.

[At the coffee shop…]

Kate: Excuse me, but you look really familiar. Have we met before?

Tom: Uh, I'm not sure.

Kate: Well, how do you know Anna?

Tom: Oh, we're old friends. We grew up together. How about you?

Kate: Anna's my exercise buddy. We run together, and sometimes we play tennis. So...well, maybe I know you from work. What do you do?

Tom: I work for an advertising firm.

Kate: Oh, really? That's so cool! How did you get interested in that?

Tom: Well, I'd always loved watching commercials and looking at ads.

Kate: Really? Me, too! I used to record all my favorite commercials!

Tom: No way…You know, I'm starving. Are you up for getting a bite to eat?

Kate: Sure, great idea. What kind of food are you in the mood for?

Tom: Uh...well...uh…we could go for shabu-shabu?

Kate: Oh, well, actually, I'm not really crazy about cooking my own food at a restaurant.

Tom: Oh, that's no problem, I'm up for anything...What kind of food do you like?

Kate: Well, this might seem kind of boring, but what I really love most is pasta.

Tom: You're kidding! Pasta is just about all I eat!

Kate: Wait a minute....now I know why you look familiar. Aren't you Eric Martino's old roommate? The one who eats nothing but pasta?

Tom: Yeah, I am. But how did you know that? Have we...

Kate: He's my brother's best friend. He's posted lots of pictures of you on Facebook...and he always used to complain that all you ever cooked was pasta.

Tom: Wow, small world!

Kate: Hey, let's text him a picture of the two of us. That'll surprise him!

LESSON 9

Conversation, Part C

Julia: Hey, Eric. I'm starving. Do you want to have lunch?

Eric: Yeah, I'm hungry, too. Where do you want to go?

Julia: Great. How about the burger place downtown?

Eric: Oh, well, I don't really like to eat junk food. And actually, I'm a vegan.

Julia: What do you mean by "vegan"? Is that the same thing as a vegetarian?

Eric: It's not exactly the same thing. A vegan is a person who doesn't eat any animal products, not even milk or cheese.

Julia: Oh, I see. Where would you like to eat?

Eric: I've been wanting to try the new sandwich place. All their food is organic and locally sourced. It's supposed to be really good.

Julia: I'm not sure what you mean by "locally sourced." I've never heard of that before.

Eric: What I mean is all the food comes from local farms.

Julia: Oh, well, that sounds great.

LESSON 10

Listening, Part A and B

A: Hey, Sandra. Wow, your room is even messier than usual! What's going on in here?

B: Hi, Tina. I know, it's a huge mess! Since it always takes me forever to decide what to wear in the morning, I decided to tidy up my closet. I thought it might make it easier to find things.

A: That's great! But it doesn't look like you've gotten very far. There are clothes all over the room! What happened?

B: Well, as I was organizing, I started finding clothes that I'd forgotten I had. Some were brand new and still had tags on them! So since I didn't remember what the clothes looked like, I decided to try them all on.

A: I guess that makes sense. But why is the rest of your room such a mess?

B: Well, once I started cleaning my closet, I wanted to clean my whole room. I decided to organize my desk because I can never find anything in there.

A: Good for you! But there are papers everywhere now. What are you going to do?

B: I guess I have to get some file folders and file everything.

A: That's a good idea. But what about your bookshelf? How come all of your books are on the floor?

B: I bought some new books yesterday, so I decided to try to make room on my bookshelf for them. But I think I just have too many books.

A: I think you might have too much of everything.

B: Yeah, I think you're right. Since I have such a small room, I should get rid of the clothes I never wear and the books I've already read. Do you want to help me organize?

A: No, thanks. I think I have a class right now.

LESSON 11

Conversation, Part C

David: You look tired, Michael.

Michael: Yeah, I spent the whole night updating my website and posting on message boards. I'm exhausted.

David: Weren't you up really late the night before, too?

Michael: Uh-huh. I was up half the night watching a live stream of a concert.

David: You didn't sleep much over the weekend either.

Michael: I know. I was busy researching and writing new blog posts. I was also uploading videos to a video sharing site. You should watch my videos.

David: I'm surprised that you can even talk to me right now. Your eyes are almost closed.

Michael: I know. I should really get more sleep. I spend too much time online.

LESSON 12

Listening, Part A and B

1. A: Aren't you going to recycle that bottle?

B: I usually recycle, but it's just one bottle. There's no recycling bin around here, and I don't want to carry an empty bottle around all day, so I'm just going to throw it away.

A: But isn't it important to recycle all the plastic we use?

B: I see what you mean, but I don't think one bottle makes a difference.

A: If everyone in the world threw away one bottle a week, we would add twenty-eight million plastic bottles to landfills every month.

B: Wow, that's a lot of plastic. OK, I'll recycle this.

2. A: Are you ready to go shopping?

B: Yes, I am. Let's go. I can't wait to get some new clothes.

A: Did you bring your reusable bags?

B: I don't use those for clothes shopping. I only use them for groceries.

A: But don't you think we should reduce waste any way we can?

B: You have a point, but I don't go shopping very often. And I like the bags that I get at the department stores.

A: Do you reuse those bags?

B: Sometimes. I use them to carry gifts to people's houses and things like that.

A: Couldn't you just carry things like that in your backpack?

B: I guess I could, but I don't feel like carrying reusable bags today. Come on, let's just go.

3. A: How are we getting to the movies?
B: I can drive my car. I don't mind.
A: Why don't we take the subway? We can get it a block away from my apartment and it will drop us off right in front of the theater.
B: Yeah, but I don't feel like taking the subway. Let's just take my car. It's easier.
A: Taking public transportation reduces carbon emissions, though. Don't you think we should do what we can to cut down on greenhouse gases?
B: You have a point, but the subway takes longer.
A: That may be true, but on the other hand, there's probably going to be a lot of traffic at this time of day.
B: I guess that's true, but I'm still not convinced that public transportation is a better way to go.

LESSONS 9–12 ENGLISH IN ACTION

Maria: Good morning, Kate.
Kate: Good afternoon, you mean. You slept past noon!
Maria: I did? Wow. Well, I was up half the night. I've been really worried about climate change, so I decided to reduce my carbon footprint. And I was reading all these blogs by people who have changed their lifestyles. I guess I spend too much time online, huh?
Kate: Yeah, probably. So...carbon footprint…I should know this, but I don't really get what carbon footprint means.
Maria: Oh, well, it means...I guess...the impact that everything you do has on climate change. You know, global warming.
Kate: Oh, right. Well, I'm impressed.
Maria: Like for example, we use way too much electricity. We don't really need to have the lights on during the day. And don't you think we should use candles instead of lights at night?
Kate: Oh. You have a point, but wouldn't that be bad for our eyes?
Maria: Oh, no, I don't think so. Not if we have enough candles. I think we have some…yeah, here they are. I mean, if everyone used candles, it would make a huge difference! See! It's like turning on the lights.
Kate: Uh...right...
Maria: And we really could do a better job of recycling. You know, paperboard can be recycled.
Kate: Oh. Paperboard...What exactly is paperboard?
Maria: This is paperboard.
Kate: Um…I think there was some cereal left in that.
Maria: What have you been up to all morning?
Kate: Me? Oh, well, I've decided to try to be more productive because I've been feeling pretty stressed out lately...So now I'm getting lots of stuff done! I'm organizing all my papers...I'm listening to music… I'm chatting online…I'm doing laundry...I'm learning Portuguese...and now talking to you…all at once!
Maria: Great...good for you.

[Later that day…]
Tom: So, how are things going with your new roommate?
Maria: Oh, nothing's really changed. Kate's not a bad person, but she's just so messy! Her clutter is everywhere...I just can't stand it. And she makes so much noise!
Tom: That's a really tough situation.
Maria: Yeah. Anyway, how are things with you?
Tom: Really good, actually. I met this woman at Anna's cafe opening, and we really hit it off. I think we're going to get together this weekend.
Maria: Really? That's great! What's her name?
Tom: Kate.
Maria: Another Kate? I guess that's a really popular name these days, huh?

LESSON 13

Conversation, Part C

Juliana: I have an interview tomorrow. I'm a little nervous.
Dan: What kind of job are you hoping to get? What's your long-term goal?
Juliana: Well, I'm interviewing for the position of production assistant, but my long-term goal is to become a film director. I love movies.
Dan: Wow, that's exciting. I didn't know you wanted to work in the movies.

Juliana: How about you? What field do you like to get into?

Dan: I hope to get a job working with people. I love helping people. I'd like to work in the medical field. I want to be a nurse.

Juliana: You would be a great nurse!

Dan: Thank you! Good luck on your interview tomorrow!

LESSON 14

Listening, Part A and B.

1. A: So, Lina, tell me what would you bring to our organization?

   B: Well, first of all, I'm a self-starter. If I see a job that needs to be done, I do it. I don't wait for someone to ask me to do it.

   A: That's great. What are some of your other strengths?

   B: I'm very professional and I have good people skills. I get along with people very well.

   A: OK, that's good. Now what is your biggest weakness?

   B: Let me think. I would have to say that my biggest weakness is sometimes I'm a perfectionist, but that can be useful in certain situations. For example, last year when our accountant quit, I had to take over the accounting duties. I found several mistakes and saved my company over $1,000.

   A: That's very impressive. I have one more question for you. What is the biggest challenge you've ever faced at work?

   B: That's an interesting question. Once I had to give a presentation to a group of 50 employees. I had only one day to prepare. I was really nervous, but I prepared very carefully and my presentation went very well.

2. A: Your resume looks very impressive, Gil.

   C: Thank you very much.

   A: You have a lot of work experience, but what are some of your greatest strengths?

   C: Let's see. Well, I'm responsible. You can always count on me to get to the office on time and finish my work.

   A: Good, that's important. What other strengths would you bring to our organization?

   C: Well, I'm very detail-oriented. My work is never sloppy. Also, I'm very cooperative and I work well with others.

   A: I'm pleased to hear that. What is the biggest challenge you've ever faced at work?

   C: Well, once I had to manage ten projects at one time because my company didn't have enough managers. It was very difficult to keep all of the projects organized, but we finished all ten projects on time.

   A: That's great. What are your biggest weaknesses?

   C: Actually, I used to be very disorganized, but I took a class on organization skills, and now being organized is one of my biggest strengths.

LESSON 15

Conversation, Part C

Pam: I want to show you how to complete a sales transaction. The first thing you need to do is enter your employee code on the touchscreen. Then scan the bar code on the first item to ring it up. It's important to scan each item only once.

Ben: Yes, that makes sense. I need to make sure I don't scan it twice. Or I'll ring it up twice.

Pam: Exactly. The next step is to make sure that the customer gets the correct discount if the item is on sale. We usually have a lot of items on sale.

Ben: I see. So I have to check the discount list, right?

Pam: Yes, that's right. After you've checked on the discounts, you hit the "total" key. The total amount will appear at the top of the register. If the customer uses a credit card, your cash drawer stays closed.

LESSON 16

Listening, Part A and B

A: Today, I'm going to talk about tips for asking for a promotion or a raise at work. A lot of people feel uncomfortable asking for promotions and raises, but it's really all a part of the working world.

First, I want to talk about ways that you can prepare yourself to ask for a raise or promotion. One thing you can do is research your company's pay policies. Does your company offer a set salary increase after every year or two years? Does your company publish its pay rates? Another thing you can do is ask your supervisor or manager what you need to do in order to receive a raise or promotion. Then make sure you do the things that your boss expects you to do.

Next, let's explore how to actually convince your boss that you deserve a raise or a promotion. When you talk to your boss, don't expect to get a raise because you just moved into a more expensive apartment. Instead, it's important to discuss what you bring to the company. One good way to do this is to set up a meeting right after you've had a big achievement, like successfully completing a big project. And during your meeting with your boss, dress professionally, make eye contact, and be positive. It may also be a good idea to rehearse the meeting with a friend. That may help you to stay calm during the actual meeting.

To wrap up, I just want to say that no matter how nervous you are about asking for a raise or a promotion, you should just give it a shot. It may be a scary thing to do, but if you don't do it, how will you ever move up at work? All right. Does anyone have any questions?

B: Yes, I do. You mentioned that a company might publish its pay rates. Could you explain that further?

A: Of course. Some companies have set pay rates for the different positions in the company. These are usually pay ranges. You can talk to your human resources department to find out if this information is available. Any other questions?

C: Could you say more about rehearsing with a friend?

A: Sure. When you rehearse, you role-play your meeting. You practice explaining to your boss the reasons why you think you deserve more money or more responsibility. It can also help to switch roles. That way, when you are playing the part of your boss, you can get an idea of how he or she might feel when you make your request.

LESSONS 13–16 ENGLISH IN ACTION

Maria: Hey, Tom. How's it going?

Tom: Oh, things are great...really great. Come on in.

Maria: So, playing a game, Alex?

Alex: No, actually I'm preparing for a presentation I have to give at work tomorrow. I'm really nervous about it.

Maria: Oh, why's that?

Alex: Well, first of all, I can't stand public speaking. I've never presented to such a large group before. And to make it worse, my boss is going to be there.

Maria: So...what's wrong with that?

Alex: Oh, haven't I told you about my new boss? Well, let's see...she's a really difficult person...she's really controlling and critical.

Maria: Well, at least you have a boss.

Alex: Huh? What do you mean?

Maria: Oh, I still haven't found a job.

Alex: Really? That's too bad. What field do you want to get into?

Maria: Well, long term, I hope to have a management job...I'm pretty good at motivating people. But my short-term goal is just to get an entry-level job so I can get some experience. Anyway, enough about me. Do you want some help with your presentation, Alex?

Alex: Sure, that would be great...Maybe I can rehearse it and you can give me some feedback?

Tom: Sounds good. Go ahead.

Alex: Ok, just a minute. So, here goes: Hello, everyone. Um...today I'm going to talk about our, um, new software. First, um, I want to talk about the exciting features of the software. Next, we'll, um, explore the ways in which our product is better than the competition.

Proposing a worldwide sales and promotion strategy. So, um, our product has some really, um, terrific features. For example, um-

Tom: Wait a second, Alex, can I interrupt?

Alex: Uh, sure.

Tom: Well, that wasn't bad, but do you mind if I give you some tips?

Alex: Oh, please do.

Tom: So, the first thing you need to do is take your time. We couldn't really understand most of what you were saying.

Maria: Yeah, Alex! You can totally do this. Don't rush your presentation.

Alex: I see. I have to speak more slowly, right?

Maria: Yeah. And it's important to make eye contact with your audience. You were looking at your computer the whole time.

Alex: Yeah, that makes sense. I need to look at the people I'm talking to.

Tom: Right. And try not to say "um" so much. And one other thing; could you say more about what you actually achieved? I mean, you want to impress people, right?

Alex: So, um, you're, um, saying I need, um, to focus, um, on our um, successes?

[Three hours later…]

Alex: Notes, notes, notes…we've been practicing for three hours...don't you think my presentation is good enough?

Maria: Well to be honest…it's not perfect, but you still have time to work on it, right?

Alex: Oh, good! Can I try again? You're really great at motivating people, Maria.

Maria: No, no, no. I'm not that great at it. And maybe management isn't for me after all.

Alex: OK, guys, you're not going to believe this. I just got a text from my boss. She said she's decided to give the presentation herself!

LESSON 17

Conversation, Part C

Daniel: I'm really nervous. I have to give a presentation tomorrow. I have to talk in front of 200 people.

Anthony: Oh, you don't like public speaking?

Daniel: That's an understatement. I'm terrified of it!

Anthony: Yeah, a lot of people are. In fact, I've heard that it's one of the most common fears.

Daniel: Really? I didn't know that.

Anthony: Yeah. It's even more common than the fear of flying.

Daniel: Are you afraid of public speaking?

Anthony: No, not really. I enjoy public speaking, actually.

Daniel: What are you afraid of?

Anthony: Well, I have claustrophobia. I'm afraid of being in small spaces. I'm also uncomfortable around snakes and spiders. They give me the creeps.

LESSON 18

Listening, Part A and B

1. A: Hey, Lisa. What's wrong?

B: Hi, Ann. Oh, I'm just really stressed out right now. I'm under a lot of pressure at home. One of my roommates moved out last month. Now instead of getting a new roommate, my other roommate wants me to pay extra rent.

A: Oh, no! Why doesn't she want to get a new roommate?

B: I don't know. She didn't say.

A: Can you move to a different apartment?

B: I'd like to, but I don't have time to look for a new place because I'm so busy with work and school.

A: Why don't you talk to your roommate and find out why she doesn't want to get a new roommate? In my experience, it's always a good idea to find out the facts before you make any big decisions.

2. A: Hey, Leo. Can I talk to you for a minute?

B: Sure, what's up?

A: Well, I'm having problems with Andrew. I think he's mad at me for some reason. We were supposed to play basketball last night, but he didn't show up. I texted him to find out where he was, but he didn't text me back. And I said hello to him in the hallway today, and he didn't even look at me. I'm not sure what to do.

B: Have you tried asking him if he's angry?

A: No, I haven't.

B: Well, when I have a problem with a friend,

I always feel better after I talk to him. That way, if he's angry about something, you can clear it up. And if he's upset about something else and isn't angry with you, you don't have to keep feeling stressed.

3. A: Hey, Luna, you look really stressed out. What's wrong?
   B: I am really stressed out. I can't eat. I can't sleep. I don't know what to do.
   A: Tell me what's happening. Are you having trouble at school? Problems at home?
   B: It's work. Well, actually, it's someone that I work with. He keeps stealing my ideas. I told him about a great idea that I had last week, and he went straight to our boss and told him about it like it was his own idea.
   A: That's really unfair. Is he like that with other people?
   B: I don't know. He might be.
   A: I've found that it's really helpful to try to understand why someone is doing something. For example, think about why he might be stealing your ideas. Is he insecure at work? Is he afraid he's going to lose his job? See if you can help him become more secure with his own work, and maybe he'll stop stealing your ideas.

LESSON 19

Conversation, Part C

Alex: I'm so tired. We've had so many customers today! I think everyone in town is shopping today.

Sandra: I know! I could use a vacation. I haven't taken a trip in a long time.

Alex: Where would you go if you could go anywhere?

Sandra: If I could go anywhere, I would go to the Bahamas.

Alex: Interesting. Why the Bahamas?

Sandra: First of all, it's beautiful there. Second, I could explore underwater caves. And I could lie in the sun.

Alex: That sounds really fun. But I don't really feel like I need a vacation. I think I need a different job.

Sandra: What kind of job do you want?

Alex: If I could have any job, I would be a scientist.

Sandra: Oh, really? Why is that?

Alex: I would love to discover cures for diseases. Also, I've always loved science.

Sandra: That sounds great.

LESSON 20

Listening, Part A and B

A: Welcome back, Clara! How was your vacation?

B: Hi, Jack. Oh, it was awful. I wish I had gone to the beach with you instead of to the city.

A: Why? What went wrong?

B: Well, first of all, I never should have listened to my brother's advice about hotels. The room was dirty, and the staff was not friendly. My brother doesn't care where he sleeps, but I like a nice clean hotel with good service.

A: Where do you wish you had stayed?

B: I wish I'd stayed at the hotel I stayed in last year. It was great! Too bad I didn't have enough money for that hotel this year. If only I hadn't bought that new computer last month.

A: I'm sorry you had such a bad vacation.

B: That's OK. How was yours? Did you have a good time?

A: We mostly had a good time, but it was so hot. I regret going to South Beach in the middle of summer.

B: Yeah, South Beach is really hot in the summer. Do you wish you had gone to Baker Beach instead? You were thinking about going there.

A: Yeah, I do. Baker Beach is much cooler at this time of year. Also, I wish I hadn't stayed at the beach until Sunday night. I was so tired when I got home, and I had an early morning class on Monday.

B: Next year, let's plan our vacations more carefully.

A: Good idea. If I could do it over, I would go to Baker Beach, and I would come home on Saturday night so I could spend Sunday recovering from my vacation.

B: If I could do it over, I think I would take a totally different vacation. I would go to the mountains and go hiking and swimming in the lake. That would be much more relaxing than a vacation in the city.

LESSONS 17–20 **ENGLISH IN ACTION**

Tom: Hi, Maria.
Alex: Hey, Maria.
Maria: Hi, guys.
Tom: Want to join us?
Maria: Yeah, sure, thanks. So, how's it going?
Alex: Oh, not bad. Of course, I'm under a lot of pressure at work, as usual. I'm terrified of missing deadlines.
Maria: Your boss still getting on your nerves?
Alex: Yeah, and I have a lot of deadlines coming up.
Tom: Maybe you should try some relaxation techniques.
Alex: Relaxation techniques?
Tom: Yeah, I always feel better after I do some deep breathing. We can try it right now. Ready? OK, breathe in...breathe out... breathe in...breathe out...Feel better?
Alex: Wow, I do! That really works! Thanks! So, how are things with you, Maria? How's the job search going?
Maria: Oh, I don't know. I have a feeling I'm never going to get a job. I had three interviews last week, and I haven't heard back from any of the companies.
Tom: Really? Why is that, do you think?
Maria: Well, it seems like I'm either overqualified or underqualified for all of the jobs. I mean, I either have too much experience or not enough.
Tom: Oh, that's too bad. So, what would your ideal job be, anyway?
Maria: If I could do anything? Well, this is kind of embarrassing, but...I'd actually love to be an actor. I've always dreamed of that.
Tom: Really? I never knew that! So, why don't you do it?

Maria: Well, acting is hard to get into, you know? And I don't have much experience. I wish I'd been in some plays in high school, but I took school really seriously...I studied all the time.
Tom: Oh...so do you wish you hadn't studied so hard?
Maria: Well, not exactly, I guess...but I wish I'd gotten involved in some other activities, too.
Alex: But it's never too late, right? What are you afraid of?
Maria: Um...failure? And I'm nervous about being broke.
Tom: But seriously, I think you'd be great! Why don't you start small...like try out for a play at a local theater?
Alex: I could never do that...I'm terrified of public speaking.
Maria: I guess I could, but I wouldn't get paid.
Alex: But it would be a start, right?
Maria: Yeah, but I'd still need a day job.
Alex: Uh-huh. But at least if your day job were boring, you'd have something to dream about.
Cafe worker: Excuse me, I'm sorry to interrupt...
Maria: Oh, that's OK.
Cafe worker: But we're actually filming a commercial here in a little while. We need to ask you to leave the cafe...unless you'd like to be extras in the commercial, of course.
Alex: Extras?
Cafe worker: Yeah...the producer said they're looking for some people to just sit here and drink and talk. You'd even get paid for it!

LESSON 21

Conversation, Part C

Jennifer: So, how was the movie you saw last night? Did you like it?
Peter: It started out kind of slow, but by the end I was really into it.
Jennifer: What was it about?
Peter: It's about this woman whose life completely falls apart. In the beginning, she gets fired from her job. Then she can't pay her rent. So, she gets kicked out of her apartment.
Jennifer: Wow, that sounds really depressing.
Peter: Yeah, but it gets better. She has to live in her car because she doesn't have a place to stay. Meanwhile, someone is looking for her. He can't find her, though, because she doesn't have an address.
Jennifer: Who is this person?

Peter: It's an editor from a publishing company. A few years earlier, she had written a book and sent it to a publisher, but she had never heard anything back.

Jennifer: OK, this is starting to sound more interesting.

Peter: Eventually, the editor finds her and offers her a book deal!

Jennifer: Wow, that's great!

Peter: Yeah, it was a little corny, but it was heartwarming.

LESSON 22

Conversation, Part C

Mike: Hey, I just downloaded this new song. Listen. It's really mellow. Isn't it great? It's my new favorite song.

Carlo: It's a nice song, but I actually prefer more upbeat music.

Mike: Have you paid attention to the lyrics, though? They're really poetic.

Trina: Oh, are you guys talking about Adele's new song?

Mike: Yeah, do you like it?

Trina: It's great! She has the most amazing voice.

Carlo: I want you guys to listen to a song that I just downloaded. It's really danceable. The tune is really catchy, too.

Mike: This song is great. It has a really good beat.

Trina: Yeah, I think I'll download it, too. What's the name of the song?

LESSON 23

Listening, Part A and B

A: Hi, Allie. What are you doing?

B: I'm going through my closet and getting rid of old, outdated clothes. Do you want to help me?

A: Sure. I love doing this kind of stuff.

B: Great. I'd really appreciate the help. You always know what's stylish. OK, what do you think of this long black skirt? It goes all the way down to my feet. I've had it for a few years. Should I keep it?

A: Oh, I think you should keep it. Long skirts are always in style. These days, a lot of people are wearing long skirts. And it's always good to have a black skirt.

B: All right. I'll keep it. How about this red knee-length skirt? I bought this one about two years ago, and I've only worn it a couple of times.

A: Well, I don't know. It's a pretty color, and the current trend is to wear bright colors, but I think knee-length skirts are out of style now. I don't think you should keep that one.

B: Yeah, you're right. I'll give this one away. I also have this short skirt in blue. I've had this one for a couple of years. Is it out of style to wear short skirts?

A: No, you should definitely keep that one. It's still very stylish. I really like it.

B: OK. How about this gray jacket? It was my grandmother's. She wore it a lot in the sixties and she gave it to me last year.

A: That's really cute. It's so retro, and it's still in really good condition. Old clothes are made to last a long time. Don't get rid of that one.

B: All right. Let's see. What about this white sweater? It's really big.

A: It looks comfortable, but it's totally out of style. The current trend is to wear smaller sweaters.

B: Yeah, I know. But I really like it. I only wear it around the house, really. And it's so warm.

A: Then I think you should keep it. All your clothes don't have to be stylish. You should keep what you really like, even if it's outdated.

B: I think so, too.

LESSON 24

Listening, Part A and B

1. A: Guess what!

   B: What?

   A: Marc Allen is going to start his own line of clothing!

   B: You've got to be kidding! Isn't he a football player?

   A: Yeah! And he used to be a child actor in the nineties.

   B: Oh, yeah. I didn't realize he was into fashion.

   A: Neither did I. Apparently, his sister went to school for fashion design, and he started reading her books. That's how he got interested.

   B: That's amazing. When will his clothes be available?

A: Well, the rumor is that he'll start selling his clothes in the fall.

2. A: Wait till you hear this!
   B: What? Tell me!
   A: Do you remember last month when that guy called all the newspapers and said that he was that famous actor who disappeared 20 years ago?
   B: Yeah, I remember. He sounded crazy.
   A: Well, get this—he *is* that actor!
   B: You've got to be kidding! How is that possible?
   A: Apparently, twenty years ago, he got tired of paparazzi following him around all the time, so he let people just think he disappeared. He left his whole family and moved to a different country. He didn't want to be famous anymore!
   B: That's amazing! I guess he wants to be famous again, huh?
   A: Yeah, he ran out of money and wants to start acting again.

3. A: Have you heard the latest on the scandal at the Olympics?
   B: No, what happened?
   A: Apparently, an athlete paid some judges to give him a high score.
   B: No way! That's terrible!
   A: I know! I can't believe it!
   B: How did he get caught?
   A: Another judge overheard a telephone conversation between the athlete and the judge who took the money.
   B: That's crazy. I'm glad he didn't get away with it.

4. A: Have you heard about the child actor whose father stole all her money?
   B: You can't be serious! Did that really happen?
   A: Yeah. Her father was her manager. He managed her career and was in charge of all of her money.
   B: How did she find out he stole her money?
   A: When she turned 18, she wanted to take over her own finances. Her father wouldn't let her, so she hired a lawyer. The lawyer found out that she didn't have any money in any of her bank accounts.
   B: That's crazy. What did her father spend the money on?
   A: He spent it on expensive vacations and dinners, mostly. He also made some really bad investments and lost a lot of her money that way.

LESSONS 21–24 ENGLISH IN ACTION

Alex: Get this. You know how we have those clients visiting at work next week?
Tom: Uh-huh.
Maria: Yeah.
Alex: Well, my boss and I were supposed to take them out to dinner on Wednesday night. But this morning, she walks into my office and tells me she can't make it after all. So, now I have to take them out to dinner myself.
Maria: So...
Alex: So, what am I supposed to talk about all night? I mean, we shouldn't just discuss work the whole time, right?
Tom: Right, of course not. But couldn't you just talk about things that everyone's interested in? You know, music, movies...
Alex: Oh, come on. I don't know much about any of that popular culture stuff.
Tom: Well, just talk about music that everyone knows, like Morning People.
Alex: Who?
Maria: You've got to be kidding! You haven't heard of Morning People?
Alex: Well, no...I'm more into classical music.
Tom: Right. Well, I think you'd like Morning People. Their music is really mellow, and their lyrics are usually kind of provocative. Want to listen to some?
Alex: Yeah, sure...maybe a little later.
Maria: So...shouldn't you get up to speed on some popular new movies?
Alex: Yeah, I guess.
Maria: Well, Tom and I saw *Yesterday's Gone* last week. It was great...a real nail-biter.
Tom: Yeah! It's about this guy who loses his memory. When it starts out, he's walking around the city, totally confused. And then he meets this–
Alex: Uh, Tom?
Tom: Yeah?

Alex: Why don't I just go online and look up the plot? That way I'll remember it better.
Tom: Oh, sure, OK.
Maria: So...where are these clients from?
Alex: Oh, Brazil.
Maria: Brazil? I've heard Brazilians are pretty fashionable dressers.
Alex: Are you saying...Yeah, I know, I'm not exactly a trendsetter.
Tom: Well, it might not be a bad idea to get a few new clothes...
Alex: You're probably right. But I don't follow the fads. I mean, what's considered trendy right now? I really have no idea.
Tom: Kate is really into fashion. In fact, last week she helped me pick out some new clothes. Want to see them?
Alex: Sure, why not? What's considered trendy right now?
Maria: Hm...well, the current trend is to keep things simple. Nothing over the top.
Alex: Wow! Looking pretty chic, Tom! Kate has good taste. So, speaking of your Kate, are we ever going to meet her?
Tom: Yeah! We still have to meet her. We also have to meet your roommate, Maria.
Alex: It's just that she's been really busy at work lately. I'll introduce you to her sometime soon.
Maria: Yeah...soon. That's if we're still roommates.
Alex: All right...I gotta go. Looks like I need to do some shopping!

[At the office...]
Alex: I heard you were looking for me?
Kate: Yes. Hey, Alex. Nice outfit.
Alex: Oh, you like it? Thanks!

LESSON 25

Conversation, Part C

Airline employee: May I have your passport, please?
Nicolas: Yes, here it is.
Airline employee: Thank you. Let's see. Would you like a window seat or an aisle seat? The flight isn't very full.
Nicolas: I'd prefer a window seat, please.
Airline employee: OK. I have a window seat in row 12. Are you checking any luggage? How many pieces of luggage do you have?
Nicolas: Yes, I'd like to check two pieces of luggage.
Airline employee: OK. Here is your boarding pass. You can walk down the hall and go through security.
Nicolas: Thank you. My flight is leaving from Gate 14, right?
Airline employee: Yes, your flight is departing from Gate 14. Enjoy your flight!

LESSON 26

Conversation, Part C

Victoria: Hi, I have to transfer to Flight 734 to São Paulo. What gate does that flight leave from?
Airline employee: I'm sorry to inform you that the flight has been canceled.
Victoria: Oh, no! Can you rebook me on the next flight?
Airline employee: You just missed the last flight of the day. The next flight is in two days.
Hotel employee: I hate to tell you this, but we don't have any vacancies.
Victoria: Well, could you please recommend another hotel nearby?
Hotel employee: Sure, there are several hotels on Hotel Drive. The best thing to do is to go online.
Victoria: Thank you. I'll get online right away.
Victoria: Excuse me. Do I need a password to get online here at the airport?
Airport employee: No, but I'm afraid our network is down at the moment. We've been having Internet problems all week.
Victoria: This is not my day! Do you know of any Internet cafes nearby?
Airport employee: No, I'm sorry. I don't. But you can use my phone to find a hotel.

Listening, Part A and B

1. A: Good afternoon. Do you have a reservation with us?
   B: No, we don't. We were driving through town, and we decided that we'd like to stay and explore, so we need a place to stay for the night. Do you have any rooms available for tonight?
   A: No, I'm afraid we don't have any vacancies at the moment.
   B: Oh, that's a shame. Could you recommend any hotels nearby?
   A: Well, there aren't any other hotels in this area, but there are several hotels downtown. I can give you a list of good hotels for you to choose from.
   B: That's great. Would it be possible to use the computer in your business center to research these hotels?
   A: Of course. Our business center is on the second floor. If you are not a guest here, there is a small fee for the use of the computers.
   B: All right. Thank you very much for your help.
2. A: Good morning. May I help you?
   B: I hope so. I missed my flight to Tokyo because my cab got stuck in traffic.
   A: I'm sorry to hear that.
   B: Thank you. Could you rebook me on the next flight?
   A: Let me check on that for you. May I see your passport, please?
   B: Of course. Here you go.
   A: Thank you. I see you were on Flight 82 to Tokyo. That flight left about half an hour ago. It looks like there's a flight in three hours.
   B: Great!
   A: Well, I'm afraid that flight is full and there isn't another flight tonight.
   B: That's too bad. Would it be possible to get on a flight tomorrow?
   A: Let's see. Yes, there is a flight tomorrow morning at 8:00 a.m.
   B: Oh, that's early. I'll take it, but I'd better make sure I get here on time!
3. A: Hello, can I help you?
   B: Yes, I just got off of Flight 72 from Paris, France, and one of my suitcases is missing.
   A: I see. Do you have your boarding pass and your passport with you?
   B: Yes, here you go.
   A: Thank you. Let me check the computer. This will just take a moment.
   B: All right.
   A: Hm..., OK. I'm sorry to say that it looks like your luggage was damaged.
   B: Oh, no! How did that happen?
   A: I'm not sure, but I'll get your suitcase for you. Here it is. There's a tear at the top of the suitcase, and the handle is broken.
   B: Hmm. Would it be possible to have the suitcase replaced by the airline?
   A: Yes, of course. Please fill out this form, and the airline will send you a check for the cost of a new suitcase.
   B: OK, thank you.

4. A: Good evening. May I help you?
   B: Yes, I have a reservation here tonight, but I have a little problem.
   A: Oh, no. What's the matter?
   B: Well, my credit card was stolen this afternoon. Would it be possible to use your phone to report the theft to my bank?
   A: Of course. There's a phone on that table there.
   B: OK, thank you. Can you still check me into the hotel without a credit card?
   A: Well, we don't normally do that. Did you make your reservation with the same credit card?
   B: No, I used a different card.
   A: OK. Well, if you have two forms of identification, I can use the other credit card number to check you in.
   B: That's great! I have my passport and my driver's license right here.
   A: Excellent. I'll check you in, and you can call your bank from your room if you like.

LESSON 27

Conversation, Part C

Alicia: I'm so glad we came to London. It's such a beautiful city.

May: It really is. I can't wait to explore!

Alicia: What do you feel like doing? Do you want to take a guided tour or explore on our own? There's a bus tour that starts at noon.

May: Oh, I'd rather explore on our own. Guided tours are too crowded.

Alicia: I agree. Hm...what should we have for breakfast?

May: Do you think we should splurge or stick to our budget? This restaurant looks nice, but it's probably expensive.

Alicia: I think it makes sense to splurge. I mean, you only live once!

May: Well, that's true. In that case, let's go shopping after breakfast!

LESSON 28

Listening, Part and B

1. A: I'm so embarrassed.

   B: Why? What happened?

   A: I did something really inappropriate during my business meeting this afternoon?

   B: What did you do?

   A: Well, in my culture, it's customary to bring gifts to a business meeting, so I brought gifts to my meeting today.

   B: Well, that's nice.

   A: No, it was so uncomfortable. No one else brought gifts, and they all seemed to think it was strange that I did. It was a really awkward situation.

   B: Don't worry. I'm sure everyone enjoyed their gifts.

2. A: How was your trip?

   B: It was really fun, but I don't think the family that I visited will invite me back.

   A: Why not?

   B: Well, I guess I asked some insensitive questions while I was visiting.

   A: What do you mean? What did you ask?

   B: I asked the father how much his car cost. And I asked the mother how much money she makes at her job.

   A: Oh, yeah. That's considered to be personal information.

   B: I know. I'm not sure why I asked those questions. I guess I was just nervous.

   A: Why don't you write them an email and explain that you didn't mean to ask inappropriate questions, but that you were nervous. And thank them for letting you stay with them.

   B: That's a good idea. At least it will make me feel better.

3. A: Did you enjoy your trip?

   B: Yeah, I did. But I made a huge faux pas the day that I arrived.

   A: Oh, no! What did you do?

   B: Well, I was invited to come to a dinner at a colleague's house that evening. The email said that the dinner started at 7:00, so I arrived right at 7:00.

   A: Oops. I think that it's inappropriate to arrive exactly on time in that culture.

   B: I know that now, but I wasn't aware of it at the time.

   A: So what happened?

   B: Well, the host was still getting ready, and I was the only person there. I sat alone in the living room for an hour before anyone else showed up!

LESSON 25–28 ENGLISH IN ACTION

Tom: What's up, Alex?

Alex: Huh? Oh, I'm just doing some research.

Tom: Really? What kind of research?

Alex: You know our Brazilian clients are coming tomorrow, right? So, I really want to impress them. I'm reading this article on how to woo clients.

Tom: Oh? What does it say?

Alex: Well, it says it's really important to have a firm handshake. If you have a weak handshake, you might be seen as a poor leader.

Tom: Ah! I'm afraid that was a little too firm.

Alex: Sorry.

Tom: So, how else do you woo clients?

Alex: Well, you're supposed to copy their gestures...like if they fold their arms, you fold your arms.

Tom: Oh, I see. You've been practicing, haven't you?

Alex: You noticed?

Tom: Uh...yeah.

[At the office…]

Kate: Uh, Alex?

Alex: Yes?

Kate: Have you made dinner reservations for tonight?

Alex: Oh, was I supposed to…um, no, not yet…um…so should I stick to a budget, or do you think it would be appropriate to splurge a little…?

Kate: Oh, I think it makes sense to splurge, don't you? These are important clients, so you should take them somewhere really nice.

Alex: Sure, that's a good idea. Uh, could you recommend a good place?

Kate: How about Luigi's?

Alex: OK. Good idea. I'll call them right now. Yes…yes, I can wait…yes, I'd like a reservation for three people for tonight…7:30 if possible…the name is Alex…Great, thank you.

[Later that day...]

Kate: We're so glad to be able to work with you in person. So, to get started, why don't you tell us a little about your goals for your visit?

Luisa: Certainly. Well, first of all, I'd like to become more familiar with your company and the services you offer. Yes, and I'd like to give you some more details about the project we're planning, and talk about how we might collaborate on it.

LESSON 29

Conversation, Part C

Robert: Did you see the match?

Tristan: The match? What match?

Robert: Uh…the World Cup? The biggest soccer tournament in the world? Brazil was incredible! It was a close game.

Tristan: Oh? That's great. So, do you know what kind of car that is? I really like it.

Robert: Uh, not sure. So yeah, it was a really close match. At the end of the second half, the score was tied, so the match went into overtime. Then Brazil had this penalty kick, and…

Tristan: Did they? Speaking of overtime, did I mention how much I've been working lately? I've been working so much.

LESSON 30

Listening, Part A

A: Did you hear about the woman who broke into someone's house and stole a laptop?

B: No, what happened?

A: Well, she got arrested when she tried to sell it back to the person she stole it from.

B: Wait, did you say she tried to sell it back to the owner?

A: Yeah. She actually stole the computer from her next-door neighbor. Then she had a garage sale in front of her house where she tried to sell the computer and a lot of other stuff. The owner of the computer just walked outside his house and saw his computer on a table with a price tag on it.

B: What did he do?

A: He picked it up and started walking away with it, and she told him he had to pay for it.

B: Hold on. Did you say she told him to pay for it? Didn't she know it belonged to him?

A: No, she had never seen him before.

B: What do you mean she hadn't seen him before. He was her next-door neighbor, right?

A: Yeah, he was, but I guess he and his family had only moved in a couple of weeks earlier.

B: That's incredible. Didn't she think he might see the computer outside her house?

A: I guess not. Anyway, the guy walked away with the computer, and the woman actually called the police to come and arrest him!

Listening, Part B

B: Wait, she called the police?

A: Yeah, can you believe it? They came to her house and talked to her and the real owner of the computer. When they turned the laptop on, they found that all of his files were still on it.

B: Wow, that's amazing.

A: I know. The police arrested her and took her to jail. They also took away all of the items she was trying to sell. When they investigated, they discovered that she had stolen everything from people in her neighborhood! They also found out she's already a convicted criminal. She has been breaking into houses and stealing since she was a teenager.

LESSON 31

Listening, Part A and B

1. A: You know, I think television ads have more influence on consumers than radio ads do.
   B: Why do you think that?
   A: Well, I've heard that if you experience something with more than one sense, you remember it better. You can watch and listen to TV ads, but you can only listen to radio ads.
   B: Yeah, that's an interesting point, but I don't know.
   A: Like you know how when you read a news story and see it on the TV news, you remember it better than if you just read it?
   B: Yeah, that's a good point. Or if you read an article and then your professor talks about it, you remember the details of it better.
   A: Exactly.

2. A: I don't think there should be ads on ocial networking sites. They're not very effective.
   B: Well, a lot of those ads are chosen specifically for particular people, so they're probably really effective.
   A: What do you mean?
   B: I read somewhere that marketers get information about people from social networking sites and make sure that people get ads for things that they'll be interested in. It's called target marketing.
   A: Yeah, but sometimes I get ads for makeup and women's shoes, and I'm a single male.
   B: That's weird. I get ads that are targeted for me. For example, I like video games and soccer, and I always get ads for products related to sports and video games.
   A: Well, my sister told me that she gets ads for video games all the time, and she hates video games. I'm not sure target marketing always works like it's supposed to.

3. A: This ad drives me crazy.
   B: Why?
   A: Because of the jingle. I don't think commercials should use jingles. They're kind of annoying.
   B: I think they're really effective.
   A: You do? Why? They don't usually say anything important about the product, and I don't think they persuade consumers to buy the product. I think slogans have more influence on consumers.
   B: Well, I read an article about the effectiveness of advertising recently. It said that when people listen to the words from an advertisement, 62% of them remember the advertisement that the words came from. But 83% of people remember the advertisement when they hear ten seconds of the jingle from the ad. For example, everyone remembers that advertising jingle for ice cream that was popular when we were kids.
   A: Yeah, I still remember it.
   B: Me, too. I also read somewhere that jingles and music in advertisements can set a mood for a product. For example, if the jingle sounds happy, it can make consumers associate the product with happiness.
   A: That's fascinating.

LESSON 32

Conversation, Part C

News announcer: We're here in front of city hall today where citizens are waiting to join a town meeting about next year's budget. Everyone here has an opinion about what the city should be spending money on. Some want more money for schools. Others want better roads. Let's talk to some of them.

News announcer: Good evening. City officials are talking about spending more money on repairing the roads next year. What's your opinion on that?

Citizen 1: The way I see it, the city should spend money on improving public transportation before fixing the potholes. I tend to think that people should drive less, and they can't do that without good public transportation. We need better trains and buses.

News announcer: One of your fellow citizens believes that the city should spend more money on public transportation rather than on the roads next year. What are your thoughts on that issue? Do you agree?

Citizen 2: I wonder if we should spend any money on roads or transportation at all next year. It seems to me that the city's biggest problem right now is crime.

LESSONS 29–32 ENGLISH IN ACTION

News anchor: Today, the government approved major budget cuts. Officials announced plans to reduce spending on early childhood education.

Maria: Unbelievable. Education should always be prioritized. Money we invest in educating young kids now will be cost-effective in the long term.

Alex: Hold on. What did you say about…cost-effective?

Maria: Oh, I meant that spending money on educating young kids now will save us money in the future. For example, studies have shown that if children get a good education, they'll be less likely to commit crimes when they get older. So, what's your opinion on that, Alex?

Alex: Well, the way I see it…

Tom: Wait! Quiet, guys–they're talking about the game!

Alex: What game?

Tom: Shhh! Yes! Fluminense beat Flamengo in a blowout.

Alex: Oh, really? That's great. So anyway…

Maria: Oh, here it is again! My favorite commercial! Have you guys seen this?

Alex: Just a second. Did you really say you have a favorite commercial?

Maria: Oh, yeah, it's so funny. A bunch of people are in an elevator, and this guy walks in eating some potato chips, and then they all start singing the potato chip jingle…See, look! Look at that!

Alex: Hey, Tom, do we have any potato chips? I'm starving.

Tom: Hold on, Alex…this story looks interesting…

News anchor: In other news, a robber broke into a Cortland home last night and stole some valuable jewelry. A woman who was walking by the house witnessed the crime and called the police. The police were able to catch the thief, and arrested him at the scene of the crime. The owner of the jewelry, billionaire Lucas Urbanski, rewarded the witness with a check for one million dollars. He said that the jewelry had great value to him–it had belonged to his grandmother –and he wanted to thank the woman for saving it.

Alex: A million dollars for reporting a crime?!

News anchor: And now we have a live interview with the witness. Hello? Are you there?

Kate: Yes–hello!

Alex, Tom, Maria: It's Kate!

News anchor: So, what are you going to do with all that money?

Kate: Well, the first thing I'm going to do is quit my job.

Alex: Yes!

News anchor: That's everyone's dream, right?

Kate: Then I'm going to get my own apartment…I have a great roommate, but I've always really wanted my own place.

Maria: All right!

News anchor: Oh, your poor roommate…

Kate: Oh, and I'm going to go on a shopping spree and really splurge…I'll probably get my boyfriend the new TV he's been wanting.

News anchor: What a lucky guy!

Tom: Way to go, Kate!

Vocabulary Index

LESSON 1
face a challenge
get into…
have a setback
have an/the opportunity to…
make a change
make the decision to…
overcome an obstacle
take a risk

LESSON 2
injure
pass out
react
report
respond
witness

LESSON 3
arrogant
chew
etiquette
ignores
interrupt
leave
rude
stare

LESSON 4
awkward
confront
hang out with
keeps
pushy
put up with
resent

LESSON 5
acquaintance
buddy
ex-
former
future
old
prospective

LESSON 6
beat
catch
get a bite to eat
in the mood
swing by
try out
up for

LESSON 7
bubbly
conceited
extroverted
gregarious
insecure
introverted
sarcastic
standoffish
unapproachable

LESSON 8
connected
keep up with
participate
post
share links
tag
upload
wall

LESSON 9
junk food
locally-sourced
locavore
nutritious
organic
processed foods
vegan
vegetarian

LESSON 10
at the last minute
clutter
declutter
neat
organize
procrastinate
stick to it
tidy up

LESSON 11
blog
video-sharing site
live streams
apps
social networking sites
podcast
video chat
message board

LESSON 12
energy-efficient appliances
global warming
greenhouse gases
hybrid car
landfill
public transportation
recycling
reducing your carbon footprint
waste

LESSON 13
career path
dream job
entry-level job
long-term
position
promotion
raise
short-term

LESSON 14
detail oriented
efficient
hard worker
motivated
organized
perfectionist
professional
self-starter
team player

LESSON 15
bar code
cash drawer
code
discount
ring up
scan
touchscreen
transaction

LESSON 16
be punctual
dress professionally
eye contact
prepare
rehearse
research
resume
say negative things
stay calm
thank you note

LESSON 17
claustrophobia
fear of flying
fear of heights
fear of public speaking
fear of snakes
fear of spiders
fear of the dark

LESSON 18
deadlines
drop
meditating
misunderstanding
overworked
pressure
relaxation techniques
stressed
talk through
workload

LESSON 19
create
develop
discover
establish
explore
invent
revolutionize

LESSON 20
active social life
clique
fit in
get involved
give...a hard time
goof off
pick on
take...seriously

LESSON 21
corny
depressing
heartwarming
hilarious
moving
nail-biter
offensive
slow
suspenseful
tearjerker

LESSON 22
beat
catchy tune
danceable
melancholy
mellow
poetic lyrics
romantic
upbeat

LESSON 23
chic
fashionable
follows the fads
in
in style
modern
out
out of style
outdated
retro
stylish
trendsetter
trendy
up to date
vintage

LESSON 24
apparently
(be) with
break up (with)
(juicy) gossip
paparazzi
scandal
spotted
the latest

LESSON 25
aisle seat
board
boarding pass
carry-on bag
check your luggage
emergency exit row
gate
overhead bin
security check
terminal
upgrade
window seat

LESSON 26
canceled
damaged
down
expired
misplaced
missed
stolen
vacancy

LESSON 27
bed and breakfast
book things in advance
budget hotel
go off the beaten path
guided tour
hostel
keep your options
lounge around
luxury hotel
splurge
stick to a budget
tourist attractions

LESSON 28
acceptable
be aware of
customary
faux pas
inappropriate
inconsiderate
insensitive

LESSON 29
blowout
close
ejected
half-time
outscored
overtime
quarter
referee
shot
tied

LESSON 30
arrest
break into
criminal
force
investigate
suspicious
victim
witness

LESSON 31
advertisement
banner ad
brand
buying habit
consumer
influence
jingle
manipulate
pop-up ad
slogan

LESSON 32
budget
cost-effective
improve
increase
overcrowding
pothole
reduce
repair

UNIVERSITY PRESS

198 Madison Avenue
New York, NY 10016 USA

Great Clarendon Street, Oxford, OX2 6DP, United Kingdom

Oxford University Press is a department of the University of Oxford. It furthers the University's objective of excellence in research, scholarship, and education by publishing worldwide. Oxford is a registered trade mark of Oxford University Press in the UK and in certain other countries.

First published in 2013
2017 2016 2015 2014 2013
10 9 8 7 6 5 4 3 2 1

General Manager, American ELT: Laura Pearson
Executive Publishing Manager: Erik Gundersen
Associate Editor: Hana Yoo
Director, ADP: Susan Sanguily
Executive Design Manager: Maj-Britt Hagsted
Associate Design Manager: Michael Steinhofer
Image Manager: Trisha Masterson
Art Editor: Joe Kassner
Electronic Production Manager: Julie Armstrong
Production Artist: Elissa Santos
Production Coordinator: Brad Tucker

ISBN: 978 0 19 403041 0 Student Book 4 (pack)
ISBN: 978 0 19 403044 1 Student Book 4 (pack component)
ISBN: 978 0 19 403047 2 Access Card 4 (pack component)
ISBN: 978 0 19 403051 9 Online Practice 4 (pack component)

Printed in China
This book is printed on paper from certified and well-managed sources

ACKNOWLEDGEMENTS

Illustrations by: Bunky Hurter: 4, 28, 32, 46, 54, 64, 66, 72; Javier Joaquin: 8, 24, 36, 44, 56, 75; Gavin Reece: 3, 7, 16, 38, 69, 78.

Commissioned photography by: Richard Hutchings/Digital Light Source, Cover photo of person speaking; People's Television, Inc., all video stills and cast shot on page ii.

We would also like to thank the following for their kind permission to reproduce photographs: Cover (Rio) Stuart Dee/Photographer's Choice/Getty Images, (soccer) Ric Tapia/Icon SMI/Corbis, (man painting) Tim Pannell/Corbis, (background montage) PhotoAlto/Sigrid Olsson/Getty images, Howard Kingsnorth/Cultura/Getty images, Christopher Futcher/istockphoto.com, Fabrice LEROUGE/Getty images, PhotoAlto/Getty images, Andresr/shutterstock.com, Monkey Business Images/shutterstock.com, Ferran Traite Soler/istockphoto.com, PhotoAlto/Sigrid Olsson/Getty images; pg. 2 Tim E White/Getty Images; pg. 3 Nic Ortega/Corbis UK Ltd; pg. 5 Arne Dedert/Dpa/Corbis UK Ltd; pg. 6 Image Source/Getty Images (Marco), Tomas Rodriguez/Corbis UK Ltd (Jenny); pg. 7 Daniel Koebe/Corbis UK Ltd; pg. 9 Jupiterimages/Getty Images; pg. 13 Blend Images/Alamy; pg. 14 Corbis Cusp/Alamy (Bruno), Take A Pix Media/Getty Images (Max), Ahn/Alamy (Lia), Fancy/Alamy (Paul); pg. 15 Jeremy Hoare/Alamy (ticket counter), amana images inc./Alamy (eating), Ted Foxx/Alamy (orchestra), Gallo Images/Alamy (video games), Envision/Corbis UK Ltd (coffee shop); pg. 17 Glowimages RM/Alamy; pg. 18 Photodisc/Oxford University Press (Nina), Fabrice LEROUGE/Getty Images (Andy); pg. 19 hana/Datacraft/Getty Images; pg. 22 Multi-bits/Getty Images (Julia), Peter von Felbert/Getty Images (Eric); pg. 23 Cosmo Condina/Getty Images; pg. 25 Fancy/Alamy; pg. 26 Justin Geoffrey/Getty Images; pg. 27 Zooid Pictures; pg. 29 Brent Stirton/Getty Images (landfill), Luiz Guarnier/News Free/LatinContent/Getty Images (traffic jam), Peter Cade/Getty Images (shopping), Boomer Jerritt/Getty Images (deforestation), Alice Musbach/Alamy (three bins); pg. 33 Viktor Fischer/Alamy; pg. 34 Wavebreak Media ltd/Alamy; pg. 35 Dan Forer/Beateworks/Corbis UK Ltd; pg. 37 James Porter/Getty Images; pg. 39 ColorBlind Images/Getty Images; pg. 42 Hola Images/Alamy (Daniel), Jonny le Fortune/Getty Images (Anthony); pg. 43 Richard Vdovjak/Alamy; pg. 45 JGI/Jamie Grill/Blend Images/Corbis UK Ltd; pg. 47 Mihaela Ninic/Alamy; pg. 49 Science Photo Library/Alamy; pg. 52 Hemant Mehta/India Picture/Corbis UK Ltd (Jennifer), Image Source/Corbis UK Ltd (Peter); pg. 53 WALT DISNEY PICTURES/PIXAR ANIMATION STUDIOS/Ronald Grant Archive; pg. 55 Patsy Lynch/Retna Ltd./Corbis UK Ltd; pg. 57 Associated Press/Press Association Images; pg. 58 Alex Mares-Manton/Picture India/Corbis UK Ltd (Brian), Image Source/Corbis UK Ltd (Matt), OJO Images Ltd/Alamy (man's hand); pg. 59 Nicole Duplaix/Getty Images; pg. 62 Corbis Premium RF/Alamy; pg. 63 Walker and Walker/Getty Images; pg. 65 Miguel Pereira/Getty Images; pg. 67 Gallo Images/Alamy; pg. 68 Fancy/Alamy (Sophie), Jungyeol & Mina/Tongro Images/Corbis UK Ltd (Patrick); pg. 69 RunPhoto/Getty Images; pg. 73 SOCCER/Balan Madhavan/Alamy; pg. 74 amana images inc./Alamy; pg. 76 Juan Silva/Getty Images (Luiz), Take A Pix Media/Getty Images (Kim); pg. 77 Faber Castell/Serviceplan Group; pg. 79 Andrew Gorrier/Fairfax Media/Getty Images.

Additional photography provided by: Asia Images Group Pte Ltd/Alamy, Aldo Murillo/istockphoto.com, Neustockimages/istockphoto.com (speaking images in top border); DPiX Center/shutterstock.com (brushed metal texture in side border).

Video: People's Television, Inc. / www.ppls.tv